How Calm
Whipped Up A Storm

How one small app won a ton of PR and buzz
that helped it grow big –
and how YOU can too

Peter Freedman

Buzzly Press

*"Every app and startup should study
Peter's 10 Golden Rules of PR and Guerrilla
Marketing"*
Michael Acton Smith, co-founder of Calm

HOW
Calm
WHIPPED UP A STORM

How one small app won a ton of PR and buzz
that helped it grow big
And how **YOU** can too

PETER FREEDMAN
Foreword by Michael Acton Smith

Buzzly

First published in Great Britain in 2023

by Buzzly Press

© Copyright Peter Freedman

Contents

Foreword

Two of the biggest challenges that apps, startups and so many other brands face today are closely related.

First, it's never been more crucial to stand out in a noisy world and win the attention of your target customers.

Second, it's never been *harder* to do so.

This timely new book describes one solution to these twin problems that has worked superbly well for Calm. It then sets out the general principles and Peter's "10 Golden Rules of PR and Guerrilla Marketing" that you can apply yourself to win more than your share of attention, buzz and awareness for your own brand.

I've now been building and running startups for 25 years: ever since 1998 when I co-founded Firebox.com, the online gift and gadget retailer, with my friend Tom Boardman.

In 2007, I founded Moshi Monsters, a new kind of online world and game for children, which grew to having 90 million registered users across 150 countries – and inspired spin-offs ranging from a hit video game to a best-selling album, a full-length feature movie and, most recently, a sleep app for children.

In 2012, my friend Alex Tew and I co-founded Calm.

From tiny beginnings as a fledgling meditation app, Calm has grown to become the world's leading mental wellness brand, including the #1 app for sleep, meditation and relaxation, designed to help you manage stress, sleep better and live a happier, healthier life.

With hundreds of hours of original audio content available in seven languages, Calm has been downloaded over 100 million times, across over 190 countries.

I've seen the huge importance and value of generating PR, media coverage and buzz in all these businesses – but never more so than with Calm.

I wish I'd been able to read this book when I was starting any of the businesses I've just mentioned.

When Alex and I wanted to start raising Calm's profile, Susan MacTavish Best, a mutual friend in San Francisco, recommended Peter – and we're so glad she did.

I've worked with many PR folks in my career but Peter is by far the best and most creative. He is brilliant – a great idea generator, communicator, cajoler, organizer and all-round superstar.

He takes an unorthodox approach to PR and guerrilla marketing, which is exactly what's needed when everyone in the same space is battling for attention and using much the same strategies and tactics to try and achieve it.

People who know how to do what Peter does – how to build a brand virally and organically and how to generate the sort of buzz that he has for Calm – are incredibly rare. I say that as someone who has spent long years searching for them and ended up coming to the conclusion that they're extremely hard to find.

When you find one, you should grab them if you can or, at least, read and listen to what they have to say.

When Peter first sent me a draft of what was, at that point, merely a long blog post on the work that he had done for Calm, I emailed him back saying how much I'd enjoyed reading it and the chance to recall all the weird and wonderfully creative ideas it described.

And I then added the words, "This post could even be a book."

I'm delighted that the blog post that I first read has now been greatly expanded and become the book you are about to read.

Every app, startup and countless others should study Peter's "10 Golden Rules of PR and Guerrilla Marketing", as well as his advice on the secrets and benefits of creating a buzzy, talked-about brand.

The best way to start doing so is to read this invaluable book, which I urge you to do.

Michael Acton Smith
Co-founder of Calm

Introduction

This short book is for anyone who runs or markets an app – or other startup, scaleup or challenger brand – and wants to generate a ton of buzz, coverage and attention but without having a ton of money to do so.

Then again, even if you *do* have a ton of money, it's much tougher these days than once to win the attention of your target customers.

This book, therefore, is *also* for those who run or market apps, startups, scaleups and challenger brands that *do* have a meaningful budget and still need or want to generate more buzz and attention than they are currently managing.

Money on its own is no longer enough. Even those who do have it also need to understand and use the sort of PR and guerrilla marketing techniques that I outline in these pages.

This book is at least two things: part case study and part how-to book.

First, it's a case study of how one small app won way more than its fair share of buzz, coverage and attention by outdoing its rivals and others in the overlapping areas of what are variously called PR, guerrilla marketing, viral marketing, buzz marketing, brand marketing and brand-building.

Second, though, and perhaps even more, it's also a guide to how to do the same or similar yourself by applying the underlying lessons and principles that I have sought to extract – mainly from this one case study but also with some references to my work for other apps and startups.

In fact, I've used the book to outline what I call "The 10 Golden Rules of PR and Guerrilla Marketing", that I hope will resonate and prove useful for those trying to win attention for their own apps and startups.

The heart of the book comprises 10 separate chapters, each outlining one of these 10 rules, with the help of examples and case studies.

Like the book itself, most of these chapters are short by conventional standards – but some are much shorter than others, and one or two are so short that they barely deserve the name.

This book is based largely on my experience working for Calm, the now well-known meditation, sleep and mental wellness brand, from late 2016, when its global empire comprised nine staff in a one-bed San Francisco apartment, to early 2020 and intermittently thereafter.

It's based in particular on the work I did for Calm from late 2016 to early 2019, when Calm announced the completion of a Series B fundraising round of $88M, at a valuation of $1BN, making Calm the world's first mental health unicorn and marking the start of a new phase in Calm's story.

It's based, in short, on how Calm won a ton of buzz without a ton of money – in the days before it became a larger, much better-funded company.

But it also draws, more indirectly, on my experience, and what I learnt working for other startups and apps – from Craigslist to Lulu to Badoo – for a dozen years before then and was able to bring to winning attention for Calm; and finally also on a few thing that I learnt in the process.

I'm the founder and Director of Thinking of Think Inc, a creative PR and guerrilla marketing agency. I help funded startups, scaleups and challenger brands grow faster and get more buzz for their buck by winning them global attention with quirky ideas that spread virally. I have been doing so now for 18 years.

I've worked for everyone from Calm, on and off since 2016, to Craigslist, for 11 years in both the US and UK, and many other apps and startups.

"What Peter Freedman does is unique," says Amit Shafrir, who was the President of the dating app Badoo during the years I worked for it. "He is a master at creating online buzz, which spreads globally. He has shown so repeatedly for big brands, like Craigslist and Badoo."

In the early days of Think Inc, I did broadly what I still do, but without really knowing what it was that I *was* doing – or how. It was all intuitive.

After a while, though, I decided I'd better try to work out what I was doing. I therefore set out to unpack the process, with the aim of reverse engineering it, so that I could have a better chance of doing it again, on a more regular basis.

This book explains the things that I worked out – and, in particular, how I applied them to generating buzz and attention for Calm.

∾

How many apps are there worldwide? No-one knows precisely.

"Today, there are over seven million apps available across iOS and Android platforms," reports *The Business of Apps* in 2023. But if you include China, Russia and beyond, other estimates top 10 million.

A 2023 study by App Annie, the market intelligence company, reported that 125,000 new apps are launched each month – over 4,000 a day; 1.5 million a year – on the Google Play and Apple App Store alone.

Whatever the total number of apps, the fact is that 99% of all apps get little, or, in most cases, no media coverage.

Most of the rest don't get much either, since it's really, really hard – and getting harder all the time – to do so and even many of those who spend money trying don't have much success.

At the same time, though, they're battling both many competitors and their biggest threat of all, which is complete obscurity.

The vast and ever swelling number of apps means that it's both more vital and tougher than it's ever been to win attention by standing out.

Indeed, the same applies these days to most brands, as Seth Godin, the godfather of modern marketing, puts it in his book, *Purple Cow*: "In a crowded marketplace, fitting in is failing. In a busy marketplace, not standing out is the same as being invisible."

In the affluent West, at least, the more fortunate live in a world of over-abundance, where there is too much of everything, and a brimming mass of endless me-too products, with little or no meaningful difference between them.

In our modern age of oversupply and information overload, when attention is the scarcest resource, there has never been more truth in the mantra, "Get noticed or die."

Many apps long relied for growth most of all on "performance marketing" or "paid user acquisition", which means buying online ads, most of all on social media like Facebook, Instagram, TikTok and Twitter/X.

This seemed for long a trusty way to acquire your first few thousand or even first few million users. But that too has become much harder and costlier.

Changes to Apple's operating system in particular, have made it much harder to track and target potential users with the same accuracy and therefore greatly increased the cost of acquiring users in this way. One startup founder told me recently that such changes have tripled his app's cost of paid customer acquisition, while another said even more starkly that his app's "engine of growth has stalled."

And besides, the customers that you "buy" in this way tend to be less loyal and so less valuable than the ones you acquire in more "organic" ways, such as through coverage, buzz or word of mouth.

Another problem with paid acquisition is that while it's true that some brands do it better than others, it's still ultimately a commodity, where the brand with the most money wins by bidding the most money and buying the most ads.

The biggest brands in any space have often raised so much money that they're bidding up the cost of the advertising keywords that their smaller rivals want too but simply can't afford.

So again, it's more difficult than ever to buy your way to your first X thousand or Y million users – and again, the brands with the most money win.

While all forms of marketing ultimately bring diminishing returns, this is probably truest of all, especially today, of paid acquisition – and helps explain why many startups eventually die from their ever costlier addiction to it.

It is *least* true, on the other hand, of the sort of creative PR, guerrilla and viral marketing that needn't cost a vast sum but which can *continue* to make yours a buzzy, happening, talked-about brand at an affordable cost – for as long as you can keeping come up with fresh ideas to do so.

Almost every startup that I speak to tells me before we've been talking long that they operate in a crowded space, with many rivals – because, well, almost every startup does. There are, for example, reported to be over 20,000 mental health apps alone.

This book describes how one small app, in a highly crowded space, used creative PR and guerrilla marketing as one of the key ways that it solved these problems – and did so noticeably better than its rivals.

This book started life as a blog post – or, at least, it grew out of a post that I wrote in 2022 about how Calm had won what one authoritative podcaster described as "a ton of buzz" that helped fuel its growth.

This is fitting since a book based on a blog is called a "blook" and one of the past projects of which I'm proudest was creating, way back in 2005, the world's first literary prize for blooks. It was called the Blooker Prize (or, in full, the Lulu Blooker Prize, after its sponsor) and ran for two years, with more global interest and attention than any of us involved had ever expected.

When I sent a draft of my post to Michael Acton Smith, co-founder of Calm, he replied along the lines that he's already described in his Foreword and suggested that the post could even become a book.

On Michael's prompting, I went away and expanded the blog post into what has become the book you're reading now.

(Next, I want to revive the Blooker Prize – which is long overdue and would, I think, do really well again – and then justify Michael's faith by entering this book for it. Would that be allowed? I need to check the rules. It could make a great story.)

I hope both that you enjoy the book and also that you find it useful.

Flash Forward:
Moments When Calm
Seemed to Have Arrived

At Nike, I'm told, they have an expression for those marketing ideas or projects that "go over the top". These are the ones that become more than just marketing campaigns and enter pop culture.

The famous Nike swoosh and the Nike tagline – "Just do it" – must both count as examples, while Nike's Air Jordan sneakers have long been a pop culture icon.

Calm's founders have talked of Calm aspiring to become "the Nike of the mind", but the fact is that Nike is much older and bigger than Calm and has long had the benefit of vastly bigger marketing budgets, coupled with great creativity.

Few brands have produced anything that's achieved anywhere near the enduring pop culture status of the Nike examples just mentioned.

You might make the beginnings of a case for Calm's Sleep Stories, alias new-fangled bedtime stories for grownups: a new category of content and culture, which Calm invented. Sleep Stories have not only gained great traction and popularity on Calm but have also inspired myriad imitators on other apps and beyond.

Such bedtime stories 2.0 – and especially those narrated by celebrities – have become, if not quite a cultural icon, then at least definitely a thing; hailed at one point by no less than *The New York Times* as a trend to note while TV's *Saturday Night Live* has produced at least two sketches that I know involving celebrities reading Calm Sleep Stories (see below).

There have, however, been moments on Calm's journey when it has at least glimpsed what Nike means by "going over the top" and becoming part of the wider culture.

The first example I can recall was an informal one, which came about 18 months after I'd started working for Calm, and its founders had first explained that their problem was that just not enough people had heard of Calm or knew that it existed.

They were talking mainly about the US, Calm's primary market, but the moment that I'm thinking of came across the Atlantic in London, when my son attended a comedy club one evening, and reported that a big part of the comedian's set had been about – you won't guess – Calm.

Not only did the audience all know what this comic was talking about, just as he'd assumed they would, but they also laughed at his Calm jokes – the laughter of instant recognition, with no explanation needed.

This was not a moment when a particular Calm PR or marketing campaign had entered the culture but instead one of realizing that Calm as a whole had reached a certain level of popular awareness; or, at least, in one London comedy club that night.

And I remember thinking, "Pretty cool."

The second moment came not long after, in the summer of 2018, when I spotted an article on an entertainment media site in Poland, with the following headline (here translated from Polish):

"A viewer of Baa Baa Land spends eight hours looking at ... ?"

The article beneath was previewing a forthcoming episode of the Polish version of the TV game show, *Who Wants To Be a Millionaire?* (as described below in the case study for Rule Four.)

It did so by explaining that a contestant in a forth-coming episode of the show would find themselves facing the following question:

"The viewer of the film *Baa Baa Land* for 8 hours looks at:

A: web-weaving spider

B: grazing sheep

C: knitting grandma

D: bubbling lava"

[Correct answer: B.]

I don't know if the contestant who was posed this question answered it correctly but I do know that *Baa Baa Land*, Calm's first and still only movie – an eight-hour, slow-motion epic about sheep standing in a field, doing nothing – had by then achieved sufficient profile that we'd already accepted an invitation for its inclusion in a cutting edge design and technology exhibition held the same summer in Gdynia, a port city on Poland's Baltic Coast.

Entering popular – or, indeed, avant-garde culture – in Poland had never been a key marketing objective in making *Baa Baa Land*.

But the fact that it had become the subject of a question on the Polish version of *Who Wants to be A Millionaire?* – and seemed to have gone viral everywhere from Bulgaria to Vietnam – was an indicator of the awareness it had achieved elsewhere too, including its key target markets in the English-speaking world.

But these were not the only moments.

When Harry Styles narrated a Sleep Story for Calm called *Dream With Me* in the summer of 2020, it was such a big deal that his fans crashed Calm's servers on the day the story launched.

But the moment that his Sleep Story and Calm entered wider pop culture came three months later when Styles appeared as a surprise guest on *Saturday Night Live* to read an extract from it – and no less a media outlet than the aptly named site Popculture.com was among the media that reported the event.

After portraying Joe Biden in a sketch opposite Alec Baldwin as Donald Trump in a mock Presidential debate for the forthcoming US election, Jim Carrey joked that he needed to calm down and so put on his "new Harry Styles meditation tape."

When Styles then duly appeared and started reading his Calm Sleep Story in a soothing voice, Twitter erupted and his countless fans went into rapture, with Tweets like, "A harry styles cameo on the snl [*Saturday Night Live*] premiere ... I am UNWELL," and another declaring, "Harry styles showing up in tonight's snl cold open caught me so off-guard HELP??".

When the US election that Carrey and Baldwin had been role-playing on SNL duly arrived a few weeks later, Calm again entered the cultural conversation in a different way – described more fully later in this book – by sponsoring the most stressful part of CNN's election coverage: its "Key Race Alerts", accompanied by the appearance of Calm's soothing logo.

The buzz generated by Styles' appearance on SNL relied on the sheer wattage of his global fame, combined with the surprise element of his unexpected guest appearance and, of course, with the profile and reach of SNL itself.

The buzz triggered by Calm's election night sponsorship on CNN relied on the topicality and cleverness of the idea, combined with the ability of Calm by this point in its growth to afford a national TV sponsorship of this kind.

Both ideas also had a certain playfulness and humor, by then both Calm trademarks.

Another, more fleeting moment of pop culture recognition for Calm came in early 2023, in an episode of *Family Guy*, the long-running animated sitcom.

When the show's main character, Peter Griffin, made his already highly stressful day worse by tripping over the living room rug and falling head-first into the family's home stereo system, he whipped out his phone and tried to destress himself with some positive self-talk, telling himself, "It's alright Peter, just open the Calm app."

And then later the same year, *Saturday Night Live* screened an entire sketch starring Timothée Chalamet, with a supporting role for Alec Baldwin, about a celebrity recording a new Sleep Story for Calm, in a recording session that goes awry.

Both such TV appearances felt like they could have been product placements, paid for by Calm, but neither were. They both just happened organically.

I am not sure if *Time* magazine's annual list of "*Time's* 100 Most Influential Companies" counts as part of popular culture, but when it published its annual list of such companies in 2022, Calm was on it.

"Tranquility has been hard to come by these days – which helps explain the meteoric rise of Calm, a mindfulness app that saw downloads double over the course of the pandemic," reported *Time*.

"Calm, which now has 4 million paid subscribers and a $2 billion valuation, has also been working with corpo-

rate partners to expand access to its Calm Business program, through which 10 million workers now have free access to the app as a mental-health benefit."

Calm appeared in the list alongside the likes of Apple, Meta, Amazon, Alphabet (parent company of Google), Netflix, TikTok, Microsoft, Walmart, IBM, Disney and similar.

The experience of scanning *Time's* list recalled the reaction attributed to the British amateur golfer who one year somehow found himself invited to play in golf's World Series. "I looked down the list of competitors," he reportedly said, "and I was the only person I'd never heard of."

Calm, anyway, had come a long way.

The 10 Golden Rules of PR and Guerrilla Marketing

1. TRAD / NON TRAD
   → DO BOTH
2. THINK 'SILLY'
3. EXCITEMENT PLEASE
4. BUZZ FOR BUCKS
5. CELEBRITY / WEIRD
6. GUERRILLA CONTENT
7. NEVER-ENDING LAUNCH
8. SNAPPY NAMES
9. ANGLOSPHERE
10. NEWSJACK IT

Introduction

When Calm first asked me to start working for them, in late 2016, their global empire comprised nine staff in a one-bedroom, San Francisco apartment. Their founders took phone calls in the block's stairwell and important meetings in the hotel lobby across the street.

They'd approached me on the recommendation of a mutual friend and top San Francisco PR with whom I'd worked for over a dozen years for Craigslist and Lulu.

Their problem, they told me, was that not enough people knew Calm existed. What they really needed was to raise their profile.

Twelve months later, in December 2017, Calm was named Apple's App of the Year, out of some 2.2 million apps.

A year after that, it became the world's first mental-health unicorn, with a billion-dollar valuation.

Shortly after that, it became the world's top-grossing health and fitness app.

So how did Calm achieve such transformative success in such short order?

There are many answers, starting with the fact that Calm boasted, in the form of Alex Tew and Michael Acton Smith, two exceptionally smart and talented founders, whose talents included surrounding themselves with other smart and talented people.

For a more independent opinion, however, try the one given by Vinny Pujji, partner at the New York VC firm, Left Lane Capital, in his *Business Breakdown* podcast on *Calm: The Sleeping Giant*.

Pujji asks: "What did [Calm] do that was really unique in the way they got this to become […] a very well-known brand with hundreds of millions of downloads?"

He then offers two initial answers to his own question:

The first was Calm's brilliant name and branding. "[Calm] is a perfectly […] and consistently branded experience. And as you scale further and further, brand really matters."

"The second thing they did was get a ton of PR," says Pujji. They hired people who "could make sure they were getting in the news."

This ton of PR in turn delivered the profile and awareness that Calm had so wanted, along with growing trust, downloads and links.

It also helped turn Calm into a buzzy, happening and talked-about brand that others – including Apple – noticed.

Even when I started working with Calm in late 2016, when it was still just a meditation app rather than the much larger meditation, sleep and mental wellness brand that it has become, it competed in a hugely crowded space.

I recall reading at the time – though never fact-checked – that even then there were some 2,000 rival meditation apps (compared to an estimated 5,000 plus now), including at least one, the market leader, with far more funding, staff and users than Calm.

Calm knew that it couldn't outspend its biggest rivals, but hoped it could outthink them. And that is what it did, in multiple ways.

People sometimes contact me because they've been Googling things like, "Who did PR for Calm?" or "Who does Calm's PR?" or similar and are wanting to learn more about it.

This book, therefore, is about that PR.

It describes a total of 10 Golden Rules Of PR and Guerrilla Marketing – sort of foundational principles – that I'd advise following if you want to generate more than your share of coverage, profile and buzz yourself for your app, startup or, indeed, other brand.

The 10 Golden Rules of PR and Guerrilla Marketing

1. There are two kinds of PR – and you need to do both.
2. Lighten up. Silly PR is better than serious PR.
3. "If there is no excitement ready-made, some must be manufactured."
4. Creativity gives you more buzz for your buck.
5. "These days only two things win attention: Celebrities and 'Weird'."
6. The best form of PR is content marketing – and the best form of content marketing is guerrilla content marketing.
7. The never-ending launch: one lightning bolt is not enough; you need rolling thunder.
8. Names matter: a snappy name can add huge value.
9. Think Anglosphere from day one.
10. Join the cultural conversation – with reactive, opportunistic, newsjacking ideas.

RULE ONE: There are two kinds of PR – and you need to do both

Most startups only do one of the two kinds of PR – but the smartest ones do both.

The two different kinds of PR each have various names but the names I tend to give them are:

1. **Traditional PR** – the kind of serious, grown-up, conventional and "product-led" PR, that most startups do (if they do PR at all).
2. **Non-traditional PR** – the kind of more indirect, under-the-radar, "consumer-led" PR, that few startups do, but which, done well, can be a kind of super-power.

Among the things that Calm did better than its rivals was first to understand this distinction and then, second, to do both kinds well, even though most startups only do the first, as did almost all Calm's rivals.

Calm wisely treated the two different kinds of PR as different things – and, from the start, hired two different specialists to do each of them.

My responsibility, in both the US and the UK, was non-traditional PR, mainly based on creative, quirky, offbeat and sometimes silly ideas, while the more serious, grown-up PR was handled in the UK by my colleagues at Think Inc and in the US by Morgan Oliveira, a highly talented independent PR, who played a key role in Calm's PR success.

Both kinds of PR were vital in raising Calm's profile but the quirky, offbeat kind was the kind that Calm's competitors were simply not doing, and where Calm was therefore farthest ahead of the game.

Let me expand on what I call the two different kinds of PR, how they differ and when it's best to use each of them.

So when I say that there are two kinds of PR, there are no doubt more than two. It's just that I tend to divide PR into the two kinds that I've just mentioned:

- **Traditional PR** – that most brands do
- **Non-traditional PR** – that few brands do

Startups and other brands today need to be *constantly* in front of their target audience. One flash of attention when they launch is not enough. They need instead what I describe under Rule Seven below as a "never-ending launch."

What I call "traditional PR" can work well for a traditional, one-off launch campaign, or when there's something genuinely different and newsworthy to announce. Indeed, it's often the best approach in such circumstances.

Once the launch is over, though, non-traditional PR tends to be the best way of *staying* in front of people, with idea after idea.

While traditional PR generally takes a more direct, on-the-nose, and even hard-sell approach, non-traditional PR takes a more indirect, oblique, under-the-radar approach.

Calm is just one client that I've seen win huge competitive advantage by first understanding this distinction and then acting on it by commissioning non-traditional PR – alias quirky, creative PR; viral marketing/PR or guerrilla marketing/PR, among other jargon terms – when all their rivals were still just playing it straight and only doing old-school, trad, conventional PR.

Knowing how to do non-traditional PR well can therefore be a kind of secret weapon.

Yet few startups – or, indeed, other brands – even attempt it, let alone do it well.

Why?

To help answer, let me first outline a few more key differences between the two kinds of PR – starting with the following table, offering a quick summary; and then, below, provide some further explanation and examples.

TABLE: How the Two Kinds of PR Compare

	Traditional PR	Non-Traditional PR
Relies on/Driven by	Contacts	Ideas
Focus/Starting point	Product-led	Consumer-led
Attitude/Tone	Serious, grown-up	Playful, irreverent
Approach	Direct, on the nose, hard-sell	Indirect, oblique, under the radar
Ideal for	Initial launch	All other times
Virality	Non-viral	Viral
Heyday/Perfect era	20th Century	21st Century
Reach/Impact	Local/National	International/Global
Good result	One piece of coverage	10, 20, 50 pieces, posts, etc
Great result	10+ pieces of coverage	Hundreds of pieces – or more

Traditional PR: The sort that most brands do

What I call "traditional PR" itself includes at least two sub-varieties of PR. The first product PR, where you are promoting the virtues of your product to your target consumers. And the second is business and tech PR, where you are targeting more of a business audience, via the business and tech media.

It's the first kind – namely, product PR – that I mainly focus on here.

Product PR normally involves taking a straightforward, conventional and direct, "product-led" approach.

So it starts with the product or service or brand, or whatever it is you're selling, and then tells anyone who will listen how new and different and wonderful it is.

The accompanying pitch or press release might boast a headline starting something like "Brand X Announces The Launch of Y."

This kind of PR is definitely worth doing – as *part* of things, at least – and, in the right circumstances, can not only be highly effective but also the best approach.

It works best when you've got something genuinely new and different to announce. That might be a new business, product or service; a big celebrity partnership; or, in the case of business PR, a big funding announcement or some hard business news (but even then it works better if you're already a well-known or public company rather than some obscure startup).

At its best, when you land a big piece of coverage entirely about your brand and what you're selling, traditional PR is the best PR of all, delivering the kind of attention and exposure that feels like a free ad or commercial – only far better since far more credible.

Once the launch announcement is over, though, and you've got nothing fresh to share, traditional PR has several drawbacks:

- It gives you less competitive advantage, since it's what everyone else is also doing – and in largely the same way, even if some brands may be doing it better than others.
- It can often involve *chasing* the story, hoping or pleading for a mention – as opposed to *creating* the story and therefore driving it.
- Even if it works when you launch something new, it makes it hard to *keep* making news and *keep* winning coverage, since it leaves you unable to answer questions such as: yes, the launch went well but what do we do for an encore? How do we avoid becoming last week's news?

You've shared your news. You've shot your bolt. And the media have moved on, in search of *this* week's news.

On a bad day, traditional PR feels not just "traditional" but downright old-fashioned.

And the reason it does is that it dates from – was *designed* for – another age: a quieter, less frantic and skeptical age, when we all had fewer claims on our attention and much marketing consisted of pronouncing that "Our washing powder washes whiter" or "Our car accelerates faster."

So traditional PR is pretty much what PR folks were doing decades ago: pre-Internet, pre-social media, pre most of the things that have transformed the media landscape and left us all battling a constant blizzard of information and marketing messages in our modern "attention economy".

But that's not the only problem.

The bigger problem still is that, whereas non-traditional PR has a journalistic mindset, traditional PR has, at its worst, a corporate mindset and vibe.

At its worst, when you have nothing genuinely new and interesting to share, traditional PR becomes the kind of self-absorbed, self-serving corporate guff and puff that gives PR a bad name. It makes journalists moan that PRs are a nuisance and pest, who don't have a clue and just waste their time.

At its worst, it consists of pitching stories chosen by you, the brand. not because of any reasonable expectation that they might interest or matter to your target media – or, indeed, to *anyone* except you – but instead merely because they interest or matter primarily, or only, to you the brand.

At its worst, traditional PR becomes an exercise in educating your target media to ignore you.

A journalist writing for the online women's magazine Xojane, calling herself simply "Mandy", articulated better than I just have how journalists feel about this type of PR, when she wrote a while back now as follows:

"Most of my life consists of emails telling me about the exciting new advancement in toe condom technology now available in the Alps for women in their 50s.

"Or some press release, equally as niche, hilarious, irrelevant and alienating.

"Sometimes it makes me want to go [...] "no one understands me, you guys."

Modesty fails to prevent me mentioning that the reason I enjoyed Mandy's rant even more was because it served as a preface for adding, "But other times it's simply delightful", and then going on to praise as an example of the type of stories that journalists actually *enjoy* receiving an admittedly lightweight story that I had just created for the dating app Badoo.

The headline for the pitch that Mandy went on to praise was " 'J' declared 'alphabet's sexiest letter' by online flirting study." The study in question proved scientifically, with the help of big data, that women whose first name started with the letter "J" were the most likely to land an online date.

In fact, the name Jenny ranked top among the 50 most alluring women's names in Badoo study, while Jessica ranked third, followed by Jennifer in sixth and Janet twelfth. The letter "S", represented by Sarah (third), Samantha (fifth) and Sandra (ninth) was the only other letter that came even close in online allure.

Mandy then added:

"This new study they [Badoo] put out is (and I'm actually not being sarcastic here) a pretty excellent example of a PR person getting their brand talked about by a worthless not-hard-news-journo like me. I mean, if you're going to conduct a stupid study to get press, this is how it's done, friends. Specific, funny, ridiculous. What ink-stained wretches like myself might call "a good watercooler story."

" ... Is it on the bottom of the CNN scroll yet? What about now?"

You could almost skip reading this entire book and instead simply heed Mandy's above comments, which comprise a fair summary of the message at its heart.

The difference, in short, between press releases on "advances in toe condom technology in the Alps for women in their 50s" and ones on the alphabet's sexiest letters, according to big data, is the difference between the worst kind of traditional PR and what Mandy deemed the best kind of non-traditional PR – of the sort that I will now discuss next.

Non-traditional PR: the kind that few brands do but which, done well, can be a secret weapon

This is also referred to by other terms, including:

- Creative PR
- Viral marketing
- Guerrilla marketing
- Guerrilla PR
- Digital PR
- Buzz marketing
- Media neutral ideas
- Stunts
- "PR Jim, but not as we know it"
- Gonzo marketing
- Guerrilla content marketing

One of the ways I describe it is as quirky, creative PR that spreads virally, delivering buzz, traffic, links, users and growth.

I also like the term "Guerrilla content marketing" which – as far as I know – I coined myself but is not yet one that others know, let alone use.

Whatever term you use, the overall approach of this second type of "PR"/marketing, differs from that of traditional PR in at least two main ways:

First, it takes a more oblique, indirect, under-the-radar approach than the more direct, straightforward approach of traditional PR.

Second, it takes what's known in the jargon as a "consumer-led" approach – rather than the "product-led" approach of traditional PR.

It starts not with the product or brand wanting attention but instead with the target customers and asks questions like:

- What is it that *interests* our target audience?
- In an age of skeptical consumers, information overload and a constant tidal wave of information, when attention is the scarcest resource, how can we win our audience's attention?
- And then once we've won their attention, how can we insinuate our brand inextricably into the story, so that our target customers go from not knowing we exist, let alone ever thinking about us, to doing both.

With non-traditional PR, the headline of the pitch or press release probably doesn't start with the name of the brand and may not mention it all. The brand, however, is baked into the story, in a way that makes it both integral and inescapable.

So when I commissioned the world's first testicle cookbook – as a way of getting attention for the digital publishing platform, Yudu.com, by publishing a quirky example of the sort of multimedia books that it hosted – the accompanying press release didn't even mention Yudu until way down in the fourth or fifth paragraph.

Yudu, however, was the only place on the entire web to read or check out the book and got so much traffic from the attention that the book won that it promptly crashed.

Other examples of non-traditional PR include:

- The world's first job ad for an "Emoji Translator", which sparked a global media frenzy.
- The Blooker Prize, for books based on blogs ['blooks'], already mentioned in my introduction to this book and one of many ideas that helped the self-publishing site Lulu grow seven-fold in 18 months.

The above examples all illustrate the point that non-traditional PR is not just consumer-led but also idea-driven.

The *idea* is the magic ingredient, the X factor and the secret sauce of successful PR stories. Their success relies more on the quality of the idea than on either the size of the PR budget or who the PR person has lately taken to lunch to "schmooze and booze". (I discuss this point at more length below, under Rule Four, that, "Creativity gives you more buzz for your buck.")

They are also all examples of what Seth Godin, the great guru of modern marketing, calls "purple cows". These are things or products or, in this case, pieces of content that are inherently remarkable enough that people *want* to read and write and talk and post about them; as opposed to being interrupted, cajoled or bludgeoned into doing so.

Non-traditional PR is in the business of creating purple cows, whereas traditional PR is often in the business of taking unremarkable things and trying to interest others in them by hoping – often vainly – to manage somehow to sprinkle magic PR dust on them.

In non-traditional PR, the media interest is baked in, whereas in traditional PR, it is sprinkled on; or, at least, that's the hope, since sometimes the sort of magic PR dust requested too late in the day proves to be in short supply.

Traditional PR is serious. Non-traditional PR often has a smile on its face.

Traditional PR tends to be more earnest and/or self-important. Non-traditional PR is often irreverent and playful. It wants to surprise and delight. On a good day, it can boast a kind of charm.

My aim in doing non-traditional PR is often to make others smile or laugh. One client described what I do as "Silly PR". (See Rule Two, below, on why "Silly PR is better than serious PR".) I took it as a compliment and now use the term myself.

This may be why market leaders and corporate behemoths tend to prefer traditional PR, whereas the best challenger and upstart brands are more likely to get the appeal of a non-traditional approach.

Non-traditional PR has various advantages over the traditional kind, including that:

- It provides what every marketeer wants – more for their marketing buck.
- Instead of winning just one piece of coverage at a time, it can win 10, 20, 50, 100 or more.
- It wins you more than your fair share of attention and helps you punch above your weight or budget.
- It helps you *keep* getting coverage, month after month, instead of just when you have something new to announce.

- It's memorable. Successful examples of non-traditional PR lodge in the memory and get fondly recalled years later, whereas traditional PR rarely does (unless maybe it went disastrously wrong).
- It can act like a kind of magic or alchemy, which reverses the force of gravity and turns the relationship between PR and journalist upside down. Instead of the PR chasing the journalist, suddenly it's the other way round.
- It gives you the biggest edge over your competitors, most or all of whom are unlikely to be doing this kind of PR at all.

While traditional PR can feel not just traditional but positively old-fashioned, non-traditional PR feels more geared to the modern age.

One reason that it does is that the Internet is, of course, a viral medium; something that non-traditional PR is designed to harness and leverage.

Secondly, non-traditional PR is, well, sort of PR but it's also sort of other things too.

It blurs the boundaries between marketing disciplines and straddles such disciplines as PR, social media and content marketing, plus SEO/digital marketing, viral, guerrilla, stunt and buzz marketing.

So one PR exec at Yahoo responded to some case studies of my work that I showed him by exclaiming:

"This is the Holy Grail: what everyone's looking for; the sort of ideas that drive traffic and spread around the web."

If everyone's looking for ideas that go viral, another thing they are – or *should* be – looking for are ideas that are "media neutral". These are ones designed not just for pitching to traditional media but also for sharing via both "owned media" and social media, as well as in other ways, including old-fashioned word of mouth.

If one kind of PR is much better than the other then why doesn't everyone do it?

Good question. There are various answers:

- First, it doesn't *occur* to them to do it. It's just not something they know or ever thought or think of. They don't know it's a thing.
- Second, it does occur to them to do but it doesn't appeal. If the story's not entirely about them, them, them – putting their brand front and center, as the first word in the pitch or press release – then they can't see the point or value. They just don't *get* it.
- Third, it does occur to them and they do see the point and value but they're scared to do it – since it looks sort of risky, feels kind of scary.

- Fourth, it does occur to them and they do see the value and they're not scared and they wouldn't mind doing it, but well, they don't know how.

- Fifth, it does occur to them and they do see the value and they also do know how – maybe, sort of, every once in a long while, or year or two, when they happen to have a great idea in the bath or the shower or while they're walking the dog. But they then don't know how to do it again, let alone again and again, month after month. But then few folks do.

In conclusion, there is an important role for *both* kinds of PR – both traditional and non-traditional. In the right context, on the right day, both have great value.

If, though, your launch is over and you have to pick just one kind of PR – and want to keep getting the biggest buzz for your PR buck – then non-traditional PR should be your choice.

RULE TWO: Lighten up. "Silly PR is better than serious PR."

Most startups take themselves and what they do seriously – sometimes too seriously for their own good, when they could get far more buzz and attention by lightening up a little.

I've worked with clients who responded to an idea I've suggested by saying, "I *LOVE* that idea – hilarious," but who then paused and ruled it out because, "Well, it's kind of silly, isn't it?"

My advice is: Don't knock "Silly." Silly is good. Silly is your friend. Or, as one long-term client concluded, "Silly PR is better than serious PR."

(My related advice, if you're asking, is to spend less time worrying that potential users won't take you seriously and think about you in precisely the way you want, while grasping all your key marketing messages and brand values – and more time worrying that they aren't thinking about you at all.)

The insight that Calm grasped better than its rivals was that PR doesn't all have to be straight and serious and hard-sell.

It can also be playful and fun, if not downright silly – even if, like Calm, you're ultimately tackling a serious subject, such as mental health.

Despite the seriousness of the subject, Calm was able, when it seemed right, to have a smile on its face and twinkle in its eye. When rivals were all po-faced, Calm felt able to be impish and irreverent.

The silliest ideas I did for Calm also tended to be the most successful.

Perhaps the biggest single home run was *Baa Baa Land*, the eight-hour, slow-mo movie about sheep standing in a field, doing nothing, which I've already mentioned.

I tell its story more fully in a standalone case study below, under "Rule Three: Creativity gives you more buzz for your buck," and also cite it various times elsewhere, to illustrate other points. But here's a quick summary.

We marketed it as both "the dullest movie ever made" and "the ultimate insomnia cure – better than any sleeping pill." It was another early attempt to raise awareness of Calm's growing focus on sleep rather than just meditation.

We launched it with an 87-second trailer and a poster paying an affectionate nod to the poster of the movie, *La La Land*, and ending with the reassurance that "No sheep were harmed – or consulted – in the making of this film."

Another silly idea that won loads of attention was *Once Upon a GDPR* – the world's first and only bedtime story consisting of a long and snooze-worthy extract from GDPR, the EU's new privacy legislation. (See the standalone case study on this, below.)

It launched as a Sleep Story on Calm the same week that the new GDPR law came into force, and won not just loads of international attention but considerable acclaim for being fun and different and generally cool.

We then won good coverage in the UK specifically for a Sleep Story called *A Cure For Insomnia? Cricket Explained*, which saw Henry Blofeld, a veteran English cricket commentator, explaining the sometimes baffling rules of cricket.

Ten months later came another Sleep Story, featuring John McEnroe, the one-time bad boy and superbrat of world tennis, merely *reading* the rules of tennis, in an even sillier – and still more successful – Sleep Story called *But Seriously, the Rules of Tennis*.

By pairing their narrators with an amusingly silly subject, both Sleep Stories won far more coverage than they would have done with a serious subject instead. (See the standalone case study on both Sleep Stories, below, under "Rule Five": "Only two things win attention: celebrities and 'weird'.")

"Make your reader smile and you've built a bridge of connection," wrote Robert Collier, the bestselling author and copywriter in the first half of the last century. "Make them laugh and you've paved a path to conversion."

David Ogilvy, the iconic ad man from the second half of the last century, advised in a similar vein that "The best ideas come as jokes. Make your thinking as funny as possible."

More recently, the SEO software business Moz declared that "content that is truly and broadly viral is almost always funny." It then quoted a study called *From Subservient Chickens to Brawny Men* that: "Humor was employed at near unanimous levels for all viral advertisements. Consequently, this study identified humor as the universal appeal for making content viral."

PR, however, has been slower than advertising to grasp this insight and leverage it effectively.

Jimmy Fallon, host of *The Tonight Show*, may not work in app marketing but has summed up this approach well. "'Have fun' is my message. Be silly. You're allowed to be silly. There's nothing wrong with it."

When done well, there's a whole lot right with it.

CASE STUDY

"Once Upon a GDPR"

"Wonderfully silly, in the best possible way."

— Reporter from Alphr, the tech and lifestyle site, in response to our pitch

"Privacy Policies Are Boring. This Company's Answer Is Brilliant."

— Headline in Inc.com

Once Upon a GDPR was the title of an unusual new Sleep Story that Calm launched in response to the growing media and business frenzy around the introduction of GDPR (General Data Protection Regulation), the European Union's big new privacy legislation.

Although GDPR was a piece of EU law its approaching enactment was vexing not just European but also North American and other non-EU businesses, since any business anywhere with EU customers on its database risked hefty fines for failure to comply with the long and hugely complex new legislation.

The PR brief, as ever, was to generate coverage, buzz and awareness of Calm's growing emphasis on sleep, and in particular, for Sleep Stories, its new bedtime stories for grownups.

The idea this time came from Dun Wang, a senior executive and all-round star at Calm (who inspired the internal Calm motto that "Dun is better than perfect").

The executed idea took the form of the world's first – and still only – bedtime story comprising a lengthy and tedious extract from GDPR, launched the same week that the law came into force.

We recruited Peter Jefferson, the revered former BBC announcer, who had previously read the (famously soothing) maritime *Shipping Forecast* on BBC radio for nearly 40 years, to narrate the new story in soothing tones.

We billed the new story as both "the antidote to GDPR stress" and an exciting new insomnia cure.

Or, as our press release explained:

"Insomnia is a modern epidemic," says Alex Tew, co-founder of Calm. "The search for a cure is a new Holy Grail. GDPR may be our new best hope."

Calm's new Sleep Story, called simply "Once Upon a GDPR", invites those having trouble sleeping – either due to GDPR in particular or just life in general – to lie back, wind down and drift off to the sound of the new regulation.

"New laws aren't meant to be exciting," says Tew. "That's not their role. But GDPR could sedate a buffalo."

The result was huge, international coverage, both in Tier 1 media and every other tier – along with general buzz, amusement and praise.

The coverage made Calm the "#1 Trending App" on the US App Store on the same day that Calm's founders were attending Apple's Worldwide Developers Conference. It included hundreds of pieces of coverage, in media ranging from *Mashable*, *The Telegraph*, The Press Association (the UK's answer to Associated Press), Inc., *The Verge*, *Quartz*, *MSN* and many more.

Calm won not only coverage, buzz and awareness but also kudos for a cool and funny response to a serious and stressful subject that, at the time, was looming large.

"GDPR's Best Use So Far: Bedtime Story for Grown-Ups," declared *The New York Observer*.

But my favorite piece of media reaction was a message from a reporter on *Alphr*, the tech lifestyle and product site, who responded to our pitch by declaring, "It's wonderfully silly [...] in the best possible way," before his colleagues then published a report in praise of it.

$\sim$

Postscript: *Once Upon A GDPR* went on to become a star exhibit in a major London exhibition of conceptual art called *24/7* (at Somerset House, October 2019 – February 2020), which comprised 50 works of conceptual art on the theme of the non-stop nature of modern life.

In fact, the final exhibit in the whole show comprised two sets of headphones, hanging on the gallery wall and made available for listening to – drumroll – Calm's Sleep Story, *Once Upon a GDPR*.

So Calm's latest new Sleep Story was not just a successful piece of content marketing and a PR and marketing stunt but also, it turned out, an important new work of conceptual art. Who knew?

RULE THREE:
"If there is no excitement readymade, some must be manufactured"

So wrote Silas Bent (1882-1945), the American journalist and author, in *Ballyhoo*, his celebrated 1927 book about newspaper practices.

Bent did not intend his statement as a compliment to newspapers and how they operated but it's still good advice for startups wondering how to get attention when they have nothing new to announce and or hard news to share – in short, the natural condition of most startups, most of the time.

The first challenge for brands is to grasp what can seem like the counterintuitive fact that no-one cares about you or your brand.

The harsh truth is that not only are other people are not as interested in what you're doing as you are but few – bordering on none – are interested at all. They couldn't care less. Hard to believe, I know, but true.

This might sound obvious to you but it can't be *that* obvious, given how many folks fail to grasp this, either intellectually or emotionally. How could it possibly be true?

Those who do grasp it, therefore, have an edge. They understand that it's their job to *manufacture* interest, since none usually exists. And then they also understand that the best way to do so is usually not to try to sell to your target customers but instead to try to win their attention and affection by entertaining, amusing and making them laugh.

The second, related challenge is then to grasp that even if you did manage to get attention when you first launched, you need to *keep* getting attention, even when the launch is over. Unless you come up with something new and interesting, the media circus moves on to the next new thing.

So the question is: "Yes, the launch went well, but what do we do for an encore?" Or, "Now that we've launched, or announced our latest new feature, how do we avoid becoming last week's news?"

Answering this question was a skill that Calm mastered, while rivals didn't.

Most startups – and, indeed, most brands – struggle for an answer.

They restrict themselves to making announcements, if not corporate-sounding pronouncements. And they only do that when they have some new product or feature or executive hire that *they* consider worthy of announcing but which is often not as newsworthy as they think.

A minority of others take the trouble to *create* – and *keep* creating –new and fun ideas and stories *in order* to keep having something new and buzzworthy to keep them in the eye of their target audience.

Calm not only excelled at manufacturing such excite-ment, when none otherwise existed, but did so on a repeated basis, and reaped the benefit.

I have laced this book with examples of how it did so, including the following case study.

CASE STUDY

The "Lost" Grimm Fairy Tale: The Princess and the Fox

> **"*The Princess and the Fox* is the product of an algorithm that was fed the complete works of the Brothers Grimm, the 19th century compilers of folktales, and trained to mimic their style."**
>
> — *The Times*

> **"You might call it literary cloning. We're doing for the Brothers Grimm what *Jurassic Park* did for dinosaurs – bringing them back from the dead with modern science."**
>
> — Michael Acton Smith, co-founder
> of Calm

This was one of our early efforts to generate coverage, buzz, and awareness for Sleep Stories, Calm's new content strand of bedtime stories for grownups.

This was in early 2018, long before ChatGPT and its ilk, and when the idea of generating a new story in the style of famous but long-dead writers still seemed newsworthy, funky and cool.

And so that is what we did – produced the world's first bedtime story generated by AI. And the first new Brothers Grimm tale in 200 years.

We did so by commissioning Botnik, a community of writers and developers, to feed the complete works of the Brothers Grimm into a predictive-text algorithm that had been trained by them to mimic their style.

Once the algorithm had generated enough phrases and sentences in the style of the Brothers Grimm, Botnik's human writers stepped in and assembled the material into the rough shape of a story. In truth, therefore, the story was not just written by AI but was the product of an AI-human collaboration.

"The result," I explained on Calm's blog at the time, "is a new tale in the style and voice of the Brothers Grimm – but with the occasional surreal touch and a more soothing plot and feel than some of the scarier Grimm stories."

It told the tale of a king, a magical golden horse, a forlorn princess and a poor miller's son. A talking fox helps the lowly miller's son to rescue the beautiful princess from the fate of having to marry a dreadful prince whom she does not love.

And it all began as follows:

"Once upon a time, there was a golden horse with a golden saddle and a beautiful purple flower in its hair. The horse would carry the flower to the village where the princess danced for joy at the thought of looking so beautiful and good..."

The result was over 1,000 pieces of coverage and social posts across over 30 countries, in media ranging from BBC News and *The Times* to *The Daily Mail/Mail Online*, CNET, MSN, Yahoo, The Press Association (the UK's equivalent of Associated Press), *Quartz*, *Gizmodo* and many more.

This was also before the Calm app itself was available in any language but English but since the Brothers Grimm had been a pair of German academics, folklorists and writers and because we knew that Calm already had a lot of users in Germany, we pitched this not just in North America and the UK but also hired a small agency to pitch it in Germany too.

The bet of pitching specifically in Germany also paid off, with Tier 1 coverage everywhere from *Die Welt* ("The *New York Times* of Germany") to *Der Spiegel*, the famed weekly news magazine and site, which covered the story twice.

RULE FOUR: Creativity gives you more buzz for your buck

Or, to put this rule another way: you don't need a zillion dollars to win attention; you need a good idea

Or, another way still: the idea is the fuel in the car, the bullet in the gun, the jewel in the crown.

In our age of information overload and a constant tidal wave of marketing messages, it's incredibly hard to get attention for your brand – *except* when it's easy.

And what *makes* it easy, when it is, is a great idea.

The idea is what counts. When it's good enough, the idea is what turns base metal into gold and an ignored brand into the focus of sudden and compelling interest.

The typical relationship between a PR person and a journalist involves the journalist either ignoring the PR person or, if the latter's lucky, saying they're not interested.

If you come up with a good enough idea, however, it triggers what physicists call a polarity reversal, at least in the sense of flipping a switch on your normal relationship with the media. Instead of you having to hassle them, the media suddenly throng to you, asking with sudden new courtesy whether you might possibly consider granting the briefest interview.

It's a kind of magic.

That's why if I had to choose between spending big on a high-end PR agency and spending more on idea generation and execution I would choose the latter.

So for example, Calm wanted me to win coverage, profile and awareness for Sleep Stories, their bedtime stories for grownups that represented an important new content strand.

One of the many ways we achieved this was by creating the world's first bedtime story written by AI. I tell the fuller story of how we did so, as a standalone case study under "Rule Three" above, but here's a quick recap.

It was called *The Princess and the Fox*, alias *The Lost Grimm Fairy Tale*.

We created it by asking Botnik, a community of developers and writers, to input the complete works of the Grimm brothers into their predictive text algorithm and program it to replicate the Grimm style. And then, with a bit of human collaboration on the editing front, voilà!, the first new Brothers Grimm tale in two centuries.

The result was coverage in over 30 countries, along with global buzz and praise.

There are, as I've said, many different names for what I do. But at the heart of it, whatever the name, is a simple idea: creativity gives you more for your money, more buzz for your buck, and a good idea can win attention that money can't buy.

As Ed McCabe, a veteran American ad man, once put it, "Creativity is one of the last remaining legal ways of gaining an unfair advantage over the competition."

I gave an interview on the work that I was doing for Calm to the blog of Majestic.com, an SEO and digital marketing business which had been struck by the coverage we were getting. The resulting post was titled *Getting Creative With PR: Calm.com shows the way*.

Calm, it started by noting, had managed to get ahead despite facing "cutthroat competition" from rival apps.

"Despite this intense competition […] Calm has been absolutely crushing it, landing repeat coverage in major publications including *The Telegraph*, *The New York Times*, *Adweek*, *The Weekly Standard*, CNBC, NBC News, Fox News, *Fast Company* and the *LA Times*."

It added that Calm had been doing everything to "keep the ideas rolling", before adding, "Calm have shown through their various successful campaigns that they yield better results by getting creative with their PR and not using generic techniques."

It then quoted me summarizing Calm's approach by saying, "It's definitely helpful to have a decent budget and even more valuable to have know-how and contacts but often the most important element of all is having a good idea."

Well before I started working with Calm, and even before I began focusing on work with startups, my approach to what I did was based on the principle that it was all about the idea.

I like to think that I'd worked this out for myself but other people and conversations had definitely also helped to crystallize this opinion.

Some years ago, for example, I went to meet the PR director of a big brand, which wanted to generate attention for a forthcoming launch.

He jumped right in and explained why he'd asked to see me: "We're like a Formula One racing car," he said. "We're revving on the starting grid. We're raring to go. All we're missing is the idea. *The idea is the fuel in the car.*"

What he was referring to, of course, was the big idea for the launch – and specifically, the PR or marketing idea that would win the attention he needed.

On another occasion, I met a big marketing honcho at Heinz, the giant food conglomerate, who wanted attention for a new vegetarian line.

(As an aside, one of the ideas that I ended up suggesting to him was to open the world's first vegetarian butchery. He didn't buy the idea but, a few years later, someone else did, if not from me. And *The*

73

Vegetarian Butcher was later voted the "Coolest Dutch Brand".)

The reason I mention the Heinz conversation is that the main thing that I remember from it was the point at which the Heinz man suddenly looked impatient and said, "Let's talk about *implementation* later. What *I'm* interested in is *the idea*. The idea is what counts. *The idea is the jewel.*"

I remembered it because I remembered so agreeing with him – indeed, with both of the above folks.

They each put it differently but both were making the same point, which was that it's all very well having a product and a brand and a launch date and a budget.

But if you want attention, what's really going to make the difference is not the size of your budget or the breadth of your contacts but the strength of your idea.

The point is that everyone has a brand. Everyone – or, at least, everyone with any money – can buy ads. Everyone can shout, "Look at me!"

Everyone, however, does not have a great idea or the ability to generate one.

And in the end, the idea is what makes the difference and works the magic. The brand that gets the most attention, now more than ever, is the one with the best ideas.

Without an idea, you're just another brand, standing in a crowded, noisy street, shouting, "Look at me!"

Taking idea generation seriously – devoting time and money to it

Since good ideas are the thing that can change the game of getting noticed from impossible to easy, it's important to take seriously the job of generating ideas in the first place.

A surprising number of brands don't.

You need a process to *generate* a production line of ideas

Many brands come up with a good idea every, say, year or three, which is nice when it happens and works. But it's not enough.

You need to do so on a regular basis, month in, month out.

You need to generate and execute amusing, playful ideas that make people smile and strike them as both clever and funny – not just once in a blue moon, when inspiration happens to strike in the shower or while walking the dog, but again and again, until it becomes almost an industrial process.

It would take a separate book to explain properly *how* to achieve this and develop your company's "ideas muscle."

But the way at least to start doing so might involve anything from giving staff the time, training and encouragement to generate ideas and fostering the culture and incentives for them to do so, to setting up a company ideas scheme and allocating even some modest budget for buying in help from external creatives and thinkers.

CASE STUDY

Baa Baa Land — "The Dullest Movie Ever Made"

"It got everyone talking, including me."

— Rohit Zambre, writing about *Baa Baa Land* on *Steemit*

"And in my favorite example of savvy marketing, Calm put out Baa Baa Land (a riff on La La Land), an 8-hour film of sheep grazing in a field. The company marketed it as "the dullest movie ever" and promised it as the ultimate insomnia cure."

— www.globaldiscovery.co.uk

"The dullest movie ever made? We hope so," said the poster for *Baa Baa Land*, an eight-hour, slow-motion movie with no plot, dialogue or actors.

Baa Baa Land was – is – an extremely long, slow and uneventful movie about sheep standing in a field, doing nothing.

"*Baa Baa Land,*" announced our press release, "is a contemplative epic, entirely starring sheep. It is also an example of 'Slow Cinema', a genre of art films known for long takes, slow pace and lack of action or narrative."

Although paid for from Calm's PR budget, *Baa Baa Land* was also a piece of content marketing and probably the single most successful stunt I did for Calm.

We billed it as "The ultimate insomnia cure – better than any sleeping pill."

It was the first and still only movie produced by Calm, which became, as far as we know, the first and only app ever to produce a feature film.

We launched it with an 87-second trailer and a poster that paid an affectionate nod to the one for *La La Land.*

The result was huge global coverage, buzz, attention and praise. "It got everyone talking, including me," declared the social media site *Steemit*.

The story went viral in Bulgaria, Kazakhstan and Vietnam, among many other countries – even including the English-speaking ones like the US and UK that were our main target.

It became, as mentioned, not just the subject of a question on the Polish edition of the quiz show, *Who Wants to Be a Millionaire?* but also an exhibit in a prestigious Polish exhibition of design and technology.

It was covered by Reuters, *The New York Times*, CNN, Yahoo, *The Huffington Post*, *The Daily Mail/Mail Online* and many others.

We stopped counting after the first 1,500 or so pieces of coverage. But the truth is that it's never stopped being talked and written about since it was first announced. It has, you might say, entered the blood-stream of the Internet and the collective culture, and fresh references to it continue to surface online to this day, years after its launch.

I've mentioned that at Nike they talk about projects that "go over the top" and become more than just marketing campaigns to the point of entering pop culture.

Baa Baa Land could never claim to have done this to anywhere the same extent as the best-known Nike examples, but it was perhaps one of the ways that Calm came at least close to achieving this kind of broader awareness.

Producing an eight-hour feature film may sound more expensive than it actually was. In fact, it was shot in a single day, with a single camera by a single person, standing in a field beside a sheep farm in Essex, on the outskirts of London. Its entire "crew" comprised Garth Thomas, its talented British director, cinematographer, sound recordist, editor, location manager, key grip, third assistant camera operator and everything else.

I billed myself as the film's producer and screenwriter and, given that the film had no dialogue or commentary, I sometimes claim to be the world's highest paid screenwriter, at least on a dollar-per-word basis.

The whole thing was extremely silly and the media, social media and everyone else loved it.

It was also both simple and universal. Everyone in every country instantly understood what sheep were and represented – and instantly grasped that an eight-hour slow-motion movie about sheep sounded ridiculously dull.

To this day, it has, at the time of writing, higher viewer ratings on the movie database site, IMDB.com, than many if not most winners of the Oscar for Best Picture.

It made people smile. It made people laugh. And it made a huge number of new people aware for the first time of Calm, the most talked-about app in town.

RULE FIVE: "These days only two things win attention: Celebrities and 'Weird'"

CELEBRITY   WEIRD   WEIRD CELEBRITY

Some years ago, I was asked to raise the US profile of Lulu.com, the self-publishing platform based in Raleigh, North Carolina.

I needed to find someone on the ground in the US to do the media relations and pitching. A friend recommended a top PR woman in New York, who sounded good.

When I spoke to her and explained the situation, she replied with audible doubt, "A self-publishing website?" I sensed her shaking her head if not simultaneously inhaling through her teeth. "*That* will be tough."

"These days," she explained, "only two things get attention."

My ears perked up.

"One of them," she said, "is celebrities. And the other is ... weird."

I remember clearly that she used the word "weird" and *how* she used it because it seemed, on the one hand, sort of ungrammatical but, on the other, vivid and apt. I knew instantly what she meant.

I also remembered it because her words sparked a lightbulb moment for me.

I realized that what *I* did – what I do – was, is "weird"; or, at least, what *she* called weird but what *I* tend to think of maybe more as quirky, creative, offbeat, odd or silly and therefore amusing. But now that she mentioned it and I thought of it further, yes, also weird. But weird in a good way.

The more I pondered her observation, the truer it seemed.

It may not be 100% true, since there are also a few other, age-old things that still win attention, including fear, sex, money, conflict, controversy and human interest of various kinds.

But there was and is still a lot of truth in it.

What's more, I realized that if *I* had to pick just two things to win attention in the modern age, they would be the two she named: celebrities and weird.

Calm, indeed, did and does leverage both of these things unusually well.

So let me talk now more about each of them in turn.

Only two things win attention: one is celebrities

Celebrity partnerships and collaborations can add huge PR and marketing value. The right celebrity can help a brand ignite.

Enlisting celebrities as narrators, presenters and sometimes creators of its content has been a signature strength of Calm's – particularly in the time since it's become better known and funded and so better able to attract and afford star talent.

Recruiting celebrities, of course, is not always easy, especially your first one or two, and when you lack the money or profile to attract them.

Some brands manage so through personal contacts, or the strength of their cause, or by working with a charity or non-profit or by offering equity – or by a combination of some or all of these.

"For years, we wanted to get big stars involved in Calm, but we struggled because the app wasn't big enough," Calm's Michael Acton Smith told GQ Magazine in 2022.

"The breakthrough came when one of our investors introduced us to Matthew McConaughey and he used Calm for a children's charity that he works with. He said the results were amazing and so he was very willing to step in and voice a story that's been tremendously popular.

"Now we have a lot of celebrities, without us having any involvement, talking about how much they love Calm."

Getting celebrities on board is challenging and expensive but can make all the difference, if not turbocharge your PR. Even less-stellar celebs can add not just name recognition and profile but kudos, credibility, luster and pizzazz, all helping to sprinkle some Hollywood stardust on your brand.

When it comes to PR value and media interest, though, A-list celebrities are not just *slightly* more valuable than B- and C-listers but vastly, disproportionately so.

If, say, a less exalted celebrity reads a Calm Sleep Story or other piece of content then that's, well, nice – and users like it – but it's not generally the cause of great media excitement, especially if the celebrity concerned is unwilling to give media interviews or even anything but the blandest quotes for PR purposes.

But when Matthew McConaughey became the first A-list celebrity to narrate a Sleep Story for Calm, that *was* big news; as it was when LeBron James partnered with Calm to produce a range of content promoting both sleep and mental fitness.

When Harry Styles then narrated a Sleep Story for Calm, that was *so* big that his fans crashed the app on launch day.

The media attention you get from big celebrities, what's more, doesn't end once you've first announced their contribution. There is also then an ongoing legacy – a sort of long tail – of intermittent but continuing mentions and credibility for months or years afterwards.

Maximizing the coverage from big-name celebrities was among the many important contributions to Calm's PR made by Alexia Marchetti.

Only two things win attention: the second one is "Weird"

I wrote earlier that if I had to pick just two things to win attention in the modern age, they would be the two things named by the New York PR woman who I'd approached regarding the self-publishing site, Lulu: namely, celebrities and weird.

But what if I could only pick one thing and so had to choose between celebrities and weird?

Answer: I would choose weird, almost every time.

Why so?

One problem with celebrities is that they're in finite supply. They also tend to be expensive and sometimes demanding, or else have agents whose role and responsibility it is to be demanding and limit what their clients will do for you, while extracting as much as possible for whatever that they will do.

The advantage of weird or quirky or offbeat or silly ideas is that they're in infinite supply – and that they don't need to be expensive or to cost very much at all.

In the end, I did not end up working with the afore-mentioned New York PR woman above but found someone else, much better. Together, we won the self-publishing site Lulu a ton of PR and buzz, which helped it grow seven-fold in 18 months and expand from just the US and English to set up in six other languages.

We did so with the help of no celebrities but lots of weird, quirky, creative and sometimes silly ideas, executed on a fairly limited budget.

So what has this got to do with Calm? Well, two things, at least.

First, most of the ideas I did for Calm that generated the most coverage relied more on weird ideas than on celebrities.

Second, as Calm grew, and was increasingly able to attract and afford celebrity talent to narrate and some-times also create content, I had the dawning insight that there are not just two things that win attention, but also a third thing, even more potent than either of the first two.

The third thing for winning attention even better than the first two – celebrities *or* weird – is *both combined*

This third thing for winning attention, even more potent than the first two things – either celebrities or weird on their own – is both combined. So not just *either* celebrities *or* weird but *both* celebrities *and* weird at once.

It may even be a secret sauce of how to get attention nowadays.

Take a non-Calm example first.

If Gwyneth Paltrow and her Goop brand decide to launch a new candle with, let's say, a beautiful floral scent, that's, well, sort of – maybe, mildly – interesting, due to the celebrity involvement of Gwyneth Paltrow.

But when Gwyneth Paltrow and Goop did launch a new candle called "This Candle Smells Like My Vagina", this was conspicuously weird. And the partnership of "Paltrow + weird" duly generated huge buzz.

Next, a Calm example.

When Calm partnered with John McEnroe, the former *enfant terrible* turned elder statesman of world tennis, to narrate a Sleep Story, it could have asked him to read some traditional bedtime story. And that would have been, well, sort of nice and maybe kind of interesting.

Calm instead chose a weirder option and asked McEnroe to read a bedtime story called *But Seriously, the Rules of Tennis*, which involved him reading out – as you've guessed – the rules of tennis.

This was offbeat, unexpected and funny and won loads of international coverage. (See standalone case study below.)

Rule Five (A): If celebrities aren't A-List, it's better if they're doing something weird

I considered making this a separate, extra rule, since it's a valuable point, before deciding in the end to call it "Rule Five (A)" and incorporate it here.

The example of McEnroe reading out the rules of tennis illustrated the added PR value of a quirky approach and the advantage of having celebrities doing something offbeat, weird or amusing, rather than just turning up and showing their face.

Even with a big-ish celebrity, if they're only willing – or the brand only asks them – to show up and do something routine and unremarkable, there can be a big "So what? Who cares?" factor. This is something that brands, in their excitement at enlisting a celebrity, sometimes underestimate.

The examples mentioned above of using fictional celebrities like Ferris Bueller's droning economics teacher, Rumplestiltskin or The Big Bad Wolf, were also examples of adding PR value by having celebrities do something offbeat or amusing, since they involved both fictional celebs (Rumpelstiltskin and The Big Bad Wolf) and real celebrities (Nick Offerman and *Game of*

Thrones star, Jerome Flynn) as narrators, in both cases doing something fun, unusual and surprising.

The takeaway from these examples is as follows:

Dog bites celebrity is not necessarily news – unless it's a huge celebrity (or maybe a huge dog).

But celebrity bites dog is far more likely to be news. Even if it's not a huge celebrity.

In other words: **Celebrity + Weird > just Celebrity on its own.**

A better combination still, however, requires an even longer formula, since the best kind of weirdness is not just *random* weirdness but weirdness that feels fitting, appropriate and good "brand fit" for that specific celebrity and resonates more as a result.

But that's not all, since the best kind of fitting and appropriate weirdness should ideally go on and tick at least one further box by also being timely or topical.

The Sleep Story that Calm launched just before Wimbledon, with McEnroe reading the rules of tennis, is the one that best ticked all these boxes at once by involving a celebrity doing something not just weird but, even better, something also both fitting and topical. No wonder it did so well.

In other words, the following formula applies:

Celebrity + Weird + Fitting + Topical > merely Celebrity + Weird.

Rule Five (B): The celebrities don't even have to be alive or real – especially if they're doing something weird

Calm has also won great coverage by enlisting dead celebrities, including the Brothers Grimm and Bob Ross, the late TV art instructor and now pop culture icon (see standalone Bob Ross case study below).

The Brothers Grimm were lending their name and literary style to the first bedtime story generated by AI and the first new Brothers Grimm story in over 200 years, which together felt sufficiently novel and offbeat to generate great coverage. (See standalone case study, in Rule Three, above.)

Calm recruited Bob Ross, over 20 years after his death in 1995, after Michael Acton Smith spotted a book of Ross's quotes in a second-hand bookshop. It sparked the idea to repurpose the soundtrack of three episodes of Ross's 1980s TV show, *The Joy of Painting*, into three new Calm Sleep Stories and won huge media coverage by doing so.

Repurposing the soundtrack of an educational TV show as a bedtime story for an audio content app, and giving life after death to a bygone TV star with a growing pop culture profile among a new generation, both felt weird, in a good way, and helped the story hit home.

Calm also got some great earlier coverage from an idea of its founders Michael and Alex for producing a Sleep Story that involved the droning economics teacher from the movie Ferris Bueller's *Day Off* reading out the first chapter of *The Wealth of Nations*, the classic 1776 economics tome by Adam Smith, the Father of Economics.

Another case of using fictional celebrities to win attention was Calm's Sleep Story series of *Fairy Tales De-Stressed*, which harnessed fictional big names including Rumpelstiltskin and The Big Bad Wolf in such reimagined fairy tales as *Rumpelstiltskin Learns to Meditate* and *The Big Bad Wolf Learns Anger Management*.

This was also an example of adding PR value by having celebrities do something offbeat or amusing, since this project involved both fictional celebrities (Rumpelstiltskin and The Big Bad Wolf) and real celebrities (Nick Offerman and *Game of Thrones* star, Jerome Flynn) as narrators, in both cases doing something fun, unusual and surprising.

In time, of course, Calm has become a well-known brand and, in that sense, a kind of celebrity itself. A well-known brand announcing some news automatically gets more attention than an little-known one.

This can make life easier since Calm itself can these days now sometimes now almost provide the celebrity interest needed. Instead of Celebrity + Weird, simply Calm + Weird can by now go a long way (although Calm + Celebrity + Weird can still go even further.)

CASE STUDY

John McEnroe Reads the Rules of Tennis

Henry Blofeld Explains the Rules of Cricket

This case study in fact describes two different case studies with much in common.

They both involved asking big names linked with a particular sport to narrate a Sleep Story for Calm that aspired to lull listeners to sleep by detailing the rules of the sport in question.

They also both enabled Calm to get more value and buzz from partnerships with the celebrities concerned by asking the latter to do something not just fitting but also quirky and funny.

The first one involved a Sleep Story called *A Cure for Insomnia? Cricket Explained (to Groucho Marx)*, written and narrated by Henry Blofeld, a British national treasure, esteemed cricket commentator and renowned authority in the wider international world of cricket, even if not a name that meant much to most Americans.

The story's full title came from the time when Groucho Marx, the iconic American comedian and most famous of the Marx Brothers, was taken to a cricket match in 1950s London at Lords, the temple of cricket. After watching the match for some time, savoring the world's most languid and baffling sport, Marx felt moved to exclaim, "What a wonderful cure for insomnia. If you can't sleep here, you *really* need an analyst."

Robin Williams, Marx's fellow American and late, great comedian, captured the essence of the game when he declared to his fellow Americans, "Cricket is basically baseball on Valium."

Calm's Sleep Story consisted of Blofeld – with an accent and persona that amount almost to a caricature of an upper-class Englishman – introducing the novice to the complex laws and bewildering vocabulary of perhaps the world's most unhurried (and mindful?) sport, where a single match can last five long, lingering days and still end in a "draw" (tie).

The British media immediately got the joke – for that's what it was.

The Press Association, Britain's top national news agency, syndicated a report to media across the country, while national media to cover it ranged from breakfast TV to *The Daily Telegraph*, *The Times*, *The Daily Mail*, *The iNews* and more.

But thanks to both their love of cricket and the reputation of Blofeld, the story also won coverage everywhere from South Africa to India to New Zealand.

The second Calm Sleep Story in a similar vein came less than a year later when Aleena Abrahamian, Calm's dynamic head of partnerships, landed a partnership with American Express, which saw the latter offer Calm the services of its brand ambassador, John McEnroe, the tennis icon and legend of the game.

Instead of asking McEnroe to follow the example of Blofeld and merely *explain* the rules of the game that made his name, Calm upped the ante and asked McEnroe to narrate a Sleep Story that consisted of him simply *reading out* the rules (complete with sub-clauses). And not just the exciting ones.

"Just to be clear," I wrote on Calm's blog at the time, "the rules of tennis are not the *subject* of the story; they *ARE* the story – read aloud, in loving detail and the slow, soothing tones of one of the greatest tennis players who's ever lived."

The new Sleep Story was called *But Seriously, The Rules of Tennis*.

The joke, of course, was not just the inherent ridiculousness of a bedtime story comprising someone reading out the tennis rule book. It was also that McEnroe had been famed, especially early in his career for his temper and clashes with tennis umpires over their application of the game's rules – most famously of all the Wimbledon umpire, whose line call he disputed with the immortal words, "You *CANNOT* be serious!"

The pairing of narrator and subject matter was similar to asking Henry Blofeld to explain the rules of cricket but, given McEnroe's history and profile, an even better joke. Since the new McEnroe Sleep Story launched on the eve of Wimbledon, it was topical too. It was, as a result, far more effective for PR and marketing purposes than had Calm deployed McEnroe's services in a more serious and predictable way.

Once again, the media instantly got the joke – how could they fail? – and loved it.

CNN led the US coverage with a big piece on his new Sleep Story. With his central role in The BBC's annual TV coverage of Wimbledon, though, John McEnroe may be as big a star these days in the UK as in the US. And the UK coverage was even greater, led by big pieces in such Tier 1 national media as *The Daily*

Mail/Mail Online, The Times, The Daily Telegraph and more.

～

CASE STUDY

Sleeping With Bob Ross

"Twenty-three years after his death, Bob Ross seems to have found his true medium."

— *The New Yorker*

"Can't Sleep? Let Bob Ross Help You Find Some Happy Little Zzzs."

— *New York Times* headline

Before there were Calm Sleep Stories, there was Bob Ross, the iconic TV art instructor and cult host of *The Joy of Painting*, the long-running art show on America's PBS.

Ross was famed in his 1980s heyday for his chill vibe, giant perm and calming voice, which barely rose above a whisper.

So mellow was his manner and soothing his vocals that Ross gained a name as a one-man insomnia cure and hero to the hard of sleeping. The rhythmic swish-swash sound of his paintbrush against the canvas only heightened the calming effect.

Ross's reputation as an accidental human sleep aid had only grown since his death in the mid-nineties, thanks to his remarkable second life as an Internet celebrity, YouTube star and pop culture icon.

By the time Calm's Michael Acton Smith stumbled across a book of Ross's best-known quotes in a second-hand bookshop, Ross may have been dead for nearly a quarter of a century but he was still a celebrity, whose fame, if anything, had only grown since his death.

We therefore decided to revive three vintage episodes of his old TV show, and, after stripping away the original visuals, repurpose the soundtracks and his voice only as Calm Sleep Stories, for listening to before bed.

We helped, in the process, to bring Ross's relaxing, sleep-inducing vibe to a whole new audience. And by doing so, we seemed to strike a nerve.

The result was huge coverage, beyond our expectations, including The New York Times (at least three times), The Washington Post, The New Yorker, The Daily Mail/Mail Online (twice), Good Morning America (ABC), This Morning (CBS), Fox News, CNBC, Gizmodo,

Engadget, *Lifehacker*, *Mental Floss*, *Artnet* and hundreds more.

The story generated approaching 500 pieces of coverage and social posts (that we knew of) in countries and languages including the US, the UK, Spanish (Hispanic US, Spain, Argentina, Ecuador), the Netherlands, Argentina, Germany, Turkey, Singapore, Canada and Australia, plus Arabic, Japanese and Russian.

"Twenty-three years after his death," declared *The New Yorker*, "Bob Ross seems to have found his true medium."

RULE SIX: The best form of PR is content marketing – and the best form of content marketing is guerrilla content marketing

The work I did for Calm went by the name of "PR" and came under the budget line for PR but most of it – and almost all that succeeded best – was in fact more a form of content marketing than traditional PR.

It involved generating buzz, awareness, traffic and links by creating content conceived and designed from the start to win coverage and attention. And then making every effort both to pitch it to earned media and share it on social media, (while also expecting it to deliver value, visitors and users as owned media, whether on Calm's own blog, social channels or the app itself).

Everything from *Baa Baa Land*, "the dullest movie ever made", to *The Lost Grimm Fairy Tale*, the first bedtime story generated by AI, consisted of *content*, conceived and crafted from the off to generate buzz.

Since Calm was and is a content app, we were mainly producing content – mainly Sleep Stories – not just for use on Calm's blog and social channels but also on the app itself, for the consumption of users.

And that made it both easier and more fun.

But did the content that we were creating – in collaboration with Calm's content team – work first and best as content or as marketing?

In some cases – like our version of *The Shipping Forecast*, the soothing, late-night maritime report, or the Sleep Stories narrated by Bob Ross – it worked well, or maybe equally well, as both.

In other cases – like the "lost" Grimm Fairy Tale generated by AI or *Once Upon a GDPR*, the Sleep Story comprising an extract from the EU's lengthy new privacy legislation – it worked better as PR and marketing than it did as content.

But that was okay, both since it still worked adequately as content and since there was already so much other superb content on the app that Calm could afford to include the occasional item that added more value as marketing than as content.

If this type of marketing was called "PR" then it was a case of "It's PR Jim, but not as we know it."

It would be more accurate to call it a modern mashup of PR and content/ guerrilla/ viral/ social media marketing and – given that some clients value it most of all for the inbound links it generates – SEO marketing.

It also reflected the claim by Seth Godin, the preeminent guru of modern marketing, that "Content marketing is the only form of marketing left."

What Godin meant by this, I think, was that instead of using ads and press releases to declaim the wonders of their brand to time-poor and skeptical consumers, the only real way left for marketeers to win the attention of their target customers was by creating content that interests and matters to them, to the extent at least that they want to consume it.

In other words, the age of interrupting consumers to bombard them with commercial messages is over.

Brands today must instead *win* the attention of their target audience by generating content that *earns* it.

And so that's what we set out to do for Calm.

Walter Pater, a Victorian writer and critic, declared that "All art constantly aspires towards the condition of music."

If there is a marketing equivalent to Pater's observation I would suggest it should be that, "All marketing constantly aspires – or should – to the condition of content."

Content is not just – as the saying goes – king. It is, or should be, also the highest form and aspiration of all marketing.

This might just be a way of restating Godin's insight that content marketing is the only kind left. If so, I'd not just match Godin but raise him, by suggesting a second part to his assertion, as follows:

If all marketing constantly aspires to the condition of content, then what all *content marketing* constantly aspires to – or should – is the condition of guerrilla content marketing, the highest form of content marketing.

At Calm, we were aiming to deliver not just content marketing but what I'd call "guerrilla content marketing", a niche variety or sub-category of content marketing, which I have elsewhere defined as follows:

> *"Guerrilla content marketing is a form of marketing that involves creating unusual, unconventional, surprising and sometimes amusing forms of content for the purpose of using it to generate buzz and attention for brands via either traditional, social or other forms of media, both online and off."*

I tend to use the term "guerrilla" to describe anything that involves executing a clever or amusing idea that gives you more for your marketing buck. And I like the term "Guerrilla content marketing" to describe what I do since I'm generally aiming to create quirky, creative, often amusing content that does just that.

It would be more accurate, though, to say that my approach – and the one I took with Calm – straddles at least three marketing disciplines: PR, social media and content marketing; or four if you include digital PR and SEO link-building; or even more if you include viral marketing, guerrilla marketing, buzz marketing and stunt marketing).

Another way of describing what we did was creating "media neutral" ideas that worked across multiple media and marketing channels – including earned, owned and social media.

The term "guerrilla content marketing" is one, as mentioned, that I like to think that I invented (just in case the world needed another piece of marketing jargon), but which it would be an understatement to say, is not widely used.

Nonetheless, I think it's a useful term to describe an unusually effective niche type of content marketing and of marketing in general – and one that was highly effective for Calm.

～

CASE STUDY

The Big Bad Wolf Learns Anger Management – and Other Fairy Tales De-Stressed

> *"I pay for the Calm app just so that I can listen to @Nick_Offerman read The Big Bad Wolf Learns Anger Management every night, and every night it's worth the money."*
>
> — *@Zachanner (comedian)*

> *"'The Big Bad Wolf Learns Anger Management' by Christina Young, read by @Nick_Offerman on @calm is my new reason for living... er, sleeping."*
>
> — *@haddonkime*

Rumpelstiltskin Learns to Meditate was the first in a series of new Sleep Stories for Calm under the shared heading of *Fairy Tales De-stressed*, comprising three classic fairy tales reimagined for our more mindful, modern age.

Its two sequels and companions were respectively *The Big Bad Wolf Learns Anger Management (and Controlled Breathing)* and *The Wicked Witch of the West Discovers Mindfulness*.

The three soothing new takes on scary old tales were narrated by the celebrity voices of, respectively, Jerome Flynn, Nick Offerman and Keegan Connor Tracy.

All three new Sleep Stories were, therefore, examples of two things:

a) Collaborations between fictional celebrities (Rumpelstiltskin, the Big Bad Wolf, the Wicked Witch) and real ones (Flynn, Offerman and Connor Tracy),

... and also of

b) Adding PR value by having celebrities, both fictional and real, do something novel, different, surprising and fun.

You've heard of the *Just So Stories*, by Rudyard Kipling. Well, these were all "What If?" stories, exploring what might have happened and how some classic tales might have turned out differently if only their protagonists had harnessed the power of meditation, mindfulness and other mind tools to transform their lives.

Calm's new versions of the three stories were more than just a piece of whimsy. They were also utterly on brand and on message.

"Many characters in fairy tales are under clear stress – or else causing it to others," explained Michael Acton Smith of Calm. "They *badly* need to meditate or find other ways to change and cope. And so we wondered what would happen if they did."

The shared theme of the new tales was the power of meditation, mindfulness and other mind tools to transform our lives.

Flynn, the British star best known nowadays for *Game of Thrones,* voiced the modern makeover of Rumpelstiltskin. "If only Rumpelstiltskin had learnt to meditate as a much younger imp," he observed, "how differently his story might have turned out."

Offerman, best known for his role as Ron Swanson in the sitcom, *Parks and Recreation,* commented: "I think I've found my new calling – as a Sleep Story narrator. Directors are always telling me to pick up the pace and goose the energy. So it was fun for once to be asked to lean into my natural, deeply mellow timbre. Turns out, I'm a walking sedative."

Offerman also loved the new tale itself: "We all know the story of the Big Bad Wolf. But in this new version, you hear what happens next – when he goes on a journey and becomes... a different, *better* kind of wolf."

He becomes, in short, a cooler, calmer and altogether happier wolf.

The three little pigs, added Offerman, suggest that he starts calling himself the Big **Good** Wolf. "But he prefers the Big **Calm** Wolf. And they're down with that."

The Big Bad Wolf, in his case, becomes a walking advertisement for the power of anger management and controlled breathing.

With a little help – and some tough love – from the three little pigs, he discovers a new and better side to himself. One that he's kept hidden for too long but now wants to show the world.

The result was international coverage – from *The LA Times*, *Quartz*, *Lifehacker*, Yahoo, MSN and TV to the BBC, *The Daily Mirror*, *The Daily Express*, *The Irish Daily Mirror*, *The (Glasgow) Daily Record*, *The Times of India*, *Stylist*, *Get the Gloss* and more.

The idea and series also won both buzz and effusive praise on social media – in particular for Nick Offerman's narration as The Big Bad Wolf.

RULE SEVEN: The never-ending launch: one lightning bolt is not enough; you need rolling thunder

Or, once the launch is over, it's only just begun.

Product people in tech sometimes understand this rule better than PR folks, since it's at the heart of the "lean startup" methodology of endless testing, tweaking and new iterations, which means that their job is never finished.

Some (many?) PR folks, on the other hand, still sometimes think more in terms of doing a one-off launch for something and then ticking it off their list.

Brands today need to be constantly in front of people, but few are.

The half-life of an idea is ever shorter. One idea is not enough. You need a production line and conveyor belt of new ideas that *keep* winning fresh attention, coverage and buzz.

To switch metaphors, you don't need one bolt of lightning but rolling thunder – marketing's equivalent of Trotsky's or Mao's "permanent revolution" – a perpetual launch.

The key is to keep the ideas – large and small – coming.

If there's a secret, perhaps it's one that both Picasso and Shakespeare knew, despite neither ever having done any app marketing: that productivity and volume of output, coupled with a respectable batting average, matter more than stressing over trying to make every work a masterpiece and triumph, which you're, anyway, never going to manage.

To put it another way, prolific beats perfect.

This means therefore having the mindset, ability, budget and resources to be prolific and roll plenty of dice, place plenty of bets and throw plenty of spaghetti against the wall – and produce lots of quirky, distinctive, eye-catching ideas, even if some of them probably fail.

The aim should be to maximize creative output, while aiming for a reasonable batting average, based on an ultimately unpredictable mixture of strikeouts, base hits and home runs.

This might be called "the Picasso Principle", since it was the one exemplified by the iconic artist, whose self-belief was only exceeded by his volume of output. His own lifetime batting average wasn't even all that sensational but his sheer number of times at bat ended up delivering a dazzling tally of home runs.

Then again, everyone from The Beatles to Bob Dylan and Dolly Parton to Irving Berlin have taken pretty much the same approach. So indeed, do most of the cultural industries, from music to movies to book publishing; and so you might argue, does business in general.

Volume of output not only increases your odds of hitting home runs but also helps fuel the cumulative sense among your target customers that they just *keep* hearing and seeing and reading about your brand, until they *have* to start noticing, paying attention and checking you out.

113

Or, as the saying – attributed to Stalin, among others – goes, "Quantity has a quality of its own."

And so we kept the production line for Calm's PR rolling, generating one idea after another, including:

• A survey to rank the most bizarre insomnia cures ever. The winner was the medieval cure of smearing dog's ear wax on your teeth. Everyone from *Reader's Digest* to *Parade* and *Shape* magazine lined up to cover the story.

• Turning Britain's "strange national lullaby", the maritime *Shipping Forecast* broadcast daily since forever on BBC radio, into an unusual Sleep Story for Calm. (See the standalone case study below.) It got great coverage initially in the UK, where it was better known, but then gradually started to win coverage and interest in the US media too, as both a cultural curiosity and distinctive natural sleep aid.

• Creating a purpose-designed meditation to help fans cope with the special stress of watching a penalty shoot-out in football's/soccer's World Cup. This won coverage everywhere from the Press Association in the UK to *Cheddar News* in the US and others from Ireland to Asia.

• Getting widely syndicated coverage for a silly poll that voted golf the dullest sport to watch and the best to cure insomnia.

While most of the ideas that worked best were in some way quirky, offbeat or amusing we also had success with some that were hardly quirky at all but still hinged on coming up with a good idea to win media interest when none was ready-made.

We commissioned a survey, for example, asking respondents which night of the week they found it hardest to sleep. The landslide winner was Sunday.

The result and the reasons for it got more coverage than we had even hoped – everywhere from the *Daily Mail/MailOnline* to *USA Today* to Inc.com, which got so excited that it ran two separate articles on our study within a couple of weeks.

Almost equally straightforward was our survey on the most common sleep myths, meaning the ones that are also most widely believed. This got excellent coverage in the four countries – the US, Canada, UK and France – where we pitched it and even some, like Australia, where we didn't.

Such ideas were not conspicuously quirky or creative but they were solidly journalistic, with enough substance and interest to deliver good ROI, while sustaining the rolling thunder and perpetual launch that we needed.

The latest data suggest that the never-ending launch has become more important – and needs to be more never-ending – now than ever.

This is because the well-known marketing "Rule of Seven", which states that it takes seven exposures to a brand or product to turn a target customer into an actual customer, may now have to renamed the "Rule of 11", after recent Google studies suggesting that people now need not seven but 11 interactions with a brand before they know, like and trust it enough to purchase it.

A study by Adobe in July 2023 on "Advertising repetition: a Meta-analysis on effective frequency in advertising" raised the bar even higher by concluding that customers now need to see an ad no less than *36* times before making a purchase.

Another takeaway therefore is that persistence matters. Brand-building is a long game. You need to keep going until folks first *start* and then *keep* noticing that you're doing fun, novel and interesting things and come in time as a result to think of you as a buzzy, happening brand that they want to hang out and do business with.

Setting up a "Production studio" or "Ideas execution factory"

The biggest limiting factor in the whole process, at least in my experience, is not just the ability to generate enough good ideas but the resources to execute the volume of them that you ideally want.

If you want to be able to execute a lot of ideas then you should be thinking in terms of creating what might be called a "production studio" or "ideas execution factory", comprising a team of bright and resourceful "producers" or project managers, able to develop, project manage, produce and execute ideas.

The idea may be the jewel but execution also matters, as do the resources needed for it.

You're looking therefore for people who are good at getting things done and making things happen. They don't have to be staff, in-house or full-time. Some could just be capable juniors or interns; others part-time and freelance, or, if your budget stretches that far, come from suitable agencies.

But you want two, three, four such producers/project managers – or, as many as you can afford. This may not be what many brands actually *do* have but it's what I'd recommend if a new client told me that they wanted to create a buzzy brand and were serious about doing so.

Allocating the budget needed to *execute* a production line of ideas

I have indicated earlier in this book that becoming a buzzy brand does not rely on having huge money, which I still think is true, but it certainly helps, if possible, to have some kind of respectable budget, so that money isn't a constant limitation.

Brands sometimes think that they can't do stunts because they're too expensive and/or too risky.

It's true that when corporate brands do stunts they tend to be expensive but they don't need to be, since the success of a stunt or activation ultimately depends more on the strength of the idea than the size of the budget.

The size of budget to aim for is perhaps one that entails, on the hand, spending significantly less *per idea*, stunt or activation on average than corporate brands tend to and generally favoring cheaper ideas and stunts over pricier ones but on the other hand, spending more *overall* than would a brand doing more traditional PR.

The need for spending more *overall* is because the approach we're aiming for is different than traditional PR and producing stunts and guerrilla content tends to be costlier and more resource-intensive than traditional PR – and because we want to be able to produce a lot of it.

If, in addition, you want – as a growing number of brands do – PR and guerrilla marketing to bear some or much of the burden traditionally born by performance marketing, then you should be prepared to spend on PR and guerrilla marketing, not all, but at least some of the money that other brands are used to spending on paid acquisition.

∾

CASE STUDY

The Shipping Forecast: Britain's Strange National Lullaby

"It's so relaxing, the meditation app Calm even has [Peter] Jefferson's voice reading off a Shipping Forecast to help its users sleep."

— Mashable

The late-night *Shipping Forecast* on BBC radio is a maritime weather report, a British institution, a national treasure and an accidental natural sleep aid of rare potency.

Even though it was largely unknown in North America, Calm's largest market, we took the decision to turn Britain's "strange national lullaby" into a new Sleep

Story on Calm. After all, it had been lulling Brits to sleep for nearly a century and so was, by now, something of a proven cure for trouble sleeping.

The Shipping Forecast is a broadcast of weather reports and forecasts for the seas around the British Isles – and is delivered four times a day on BBC Radio 4.

We recruited Peter Jefferson, the former BBC continuity announcer, known as "the voice of the *Shipping Forecast*" after nearly four decades of reading it on the BBC, to narrate a special new version for Calm, complete with *unusually calm maritime conditions*.

He even added his own introduction, explaining for the benefit of beginners the forecast's history, background and special place, if not cult status, in British national life.

"*The Shipping Forecast* has been likened to a meditation, a mantra and a kind of lullaby, since for many people it is not just rhythmic, familiar and soothing but also the last thing they listen to at night before falling asleep," explained Jefferson (who also happens to be a distant relation of Thomas Jefferson, the third US President, Jefferson).

The early coverage we won for this unusual new Sleep Story, was, not to our surprise, in the British media, where we got good initial national coverage and then continued to get more.

In time, however, *The Shipping Forecast* and Calm's new version of it started to win a surprising amount of attention in the US media too – both as a sort of cultural curiosity and an unusual natural sleep aid.

It got noticed by everyone from *The Verge* to Yahoo and the popular podcast, *99% Invisible*, while *Mashable* declared: "It's so relaxing, the meditation app Calm even has Jefferson's voice reading off a *Shipping Forecast* to help its users sleep. The recording features a day of clear skies and gentle waves."

RULE EIGHT:
Names matter.
A snappy name can add huge value

There is not just power but magic in naming. In the Bible, Adam names the world, and by doing so, in a sense creates the things within it.

Did the color purple, for example, actually exist, other than as some undefined stretch of the color spectrum, until someone first defined it by naming it "purple"?

Does *anything* exist until it has a name?

Or, as Deepak Chopra, the author and alternative medicine advocate, once put it: "Language creates reality." And Wittgenstein said the same before him.

So the act of naming something previously unnamed also, in a sense, invents and gives birth to it. By virtue of its name, it becomes a thing. And a new thing, if it sounds interesting enough, has a shot at becoming news.

If it's a whole new phrase and you delete the spaces between the words and whack a hashtag in front, it could go even further and trend on social.

Phoebe Smith, for example, is a terrific travel writer, an intrepid adventurer and one of Calm's most talented, prolific and popular writers of Sleep Stories, with millions of listeners and fans.

She only started to earn the wider – global – media acclaim that she deserved when she dubbed herself, almost as a throwaway remark, a "sleep storyteller-in-residence."

We then made it official and announced her to the media as Calm's and the world's first official "Sleep Storyteller-in-residence."

We also coined the accompanying terms, "Slow Literature" (as in Slow Food or Slow Cinema) and "Slow Lit", to describe the new literary genre created by Calm's Sleep Stories. We then declared Phoebe both "the Queen of Slow Lit" and the "JK Rowling of Slow Lit."

All these new coinages further added to the buzz, media and social media interest around her.

It also helped that Phoebe was a great interviewee, whom the media loved.

But what was the biggest help in winning so much coverage and buzz for her Sleep Story and role for Calm was pitching her unique and intriguing job title, plus the various other names and nicknames that we invented around it.

(Read more details of the media attention for Phoebe Smith's rebranding as Calm Sleep Storyteller-in-Residence in the standalone case study below.)

We then used the same technique, of generating media interest largely on the basis of inventing an intriguing new name for something not itself perhaps entirely new, when we coined the word "sleep-storm-ing" to label a list of simple tips for coming up with ideas in your sleep and then published a Calm blog post asking, *"Is sleep-storming the new brainstorming"*?

The first tip was as simple, if not banal, as "Keep a notebook handy – and write down your dreams" – but "sleep-storming" as a whole sounded like some cool and funky new invention or life-hack and the media loved it.

The choice of *Baa Baa Land* as the name for Calm's eight-hour, slow-mo movie about sheep standing in a field also played a big role in its success. The name in this case did not *create* the idea in the same way as in the above examples but it undoubtedly enhanced it.

We had originally been thinking of calling it *The Big Sheep*, as in *The Big Sleep*, the classic 1946 Bogart movie based on the Raymond Chandler novel.

In retrospect, however, that would have been a mistake and a name that would have resonated with a smaller – probably older, English-speaking – audience.

It would also have worked worse internationally, since – unlike our play on *La La Land*, a more recent movie with a more international profile – the wordplay on *The Big Sleep* would have been more likely to get lost in translation, whereas *Baa Baa Land* seemed to work across the globe.

∽

CASE STUDY

Calm's Sleep Storyteller-in-Residence

> *"Phoebe Smith has just been appointed Calm's first Sleep Storyteller-In-Residence [...] Smith fell asleep listening to the audio version of her own story."*
>
> — *The (London) Evening Standard*

As well as announcing Phoebe Smith to the media as Calm's and the world's first Sleep Storyteller-in-Residence and pitching her as "the Queen of Slow Lit", we also published a blog post about her new role, did a photo shoot and made a video.

We launched a *Sleep Story Collection* of her best Sleep Stories, making her the first Sleep Story writer to get such a showcase.

"Like other such improbable but real, ultra-modern jobs as Ethical hacker, Cloud architect and Emoji translator," declared our blog, "Phoebe's new role of Sleep Storyteller-in-Residence is a job for our times – and she's the perfect person to fill it."

In addition to our retained PR consultant, we also hired, on a one-off project basis, PR specialists in both travel and, separately, books and publishing.

We pitched Phoebe to the features media, the travel media, the books and literary media, the "sleep media", and you name it – crafting different angles for each.

We also sent Phoebe on a speaking and media tour of the UK and Ireland, giving talks in local bookshops and, while in town, speaking to the local media.

The result of our efforts was huge media interest and worldwide coverage, in countries including the UK, US, Canada, India, Ireland, Australia, New Zealand, Italy, Russia, Hong Kong, Portugal, Brazil, Belgium (French and Flemish), France, Denmark, Germany, China, Thailand, Japan and Vietnam.

Major coverage ranged from a long report on *The Today Show* on NBC to *The Guardian* (twice), the BBC (multiple times), *USA Today*, *Time*, *The London Evening Standard*, *Parade*, MSN and many others.

RULE NINE:
Think Anglosphere
from day one

Whether this rule makes sense for your own brand obviously depends on what you are marketing and to whom.

Many English-speaking apps with a potential international market, however, will find organically that

– even if their marketing focus is mainly or even entirely on the US – the US comprises perhaps just two-thirds to three-quarters of their traffic, users and revenue from their top dozen or so national markets.

English-speaking countries beyond the US may easily contribute, say, 30% of such traffic and customers. The UK alone may contribute in the region of 20%, while Canada and Australia are likely to make up the top four markets.

If, therefore, you are trying to win users for, say, an English-language app with an international market, then why limit yourselves, as many do, to targeting just the US market?

Why not instead try to generate stories and ideas designed to appeal not merely to Americans but also far beyond?

Cost may be one obvious answer but – as I explain below – the extra cost involved in targeting additional Anglophone countries may be smaller than you think.

"Think global from day one" is the common advice for startup founders. But if you run an English-language app, a better version of this mantra might be, "Think Anglophone – or just 'Think Anglo' – from day one," as in, think from day one of targeting at least the global Anglosphere.

Or, if you're an app charging a subscription that is likely to be more affordable in richer countries, then target at least what might be called the "Western Anglosphere", or perhaps the "WAnglo" for short.

So the most practical advice when it comes to PR is to "Think WAnglo – as in, 'Think Western Anglosphere' – from day one."

The most practical way to do this is how Calm did it – by having PR folks on the ground and pitching your ideas in at least two key initial markets: both the US (but in fact pitching ideally both the US *and* Canada) and the UK.

What's more, is that you can pitch the same – or essentially the same – idea in both North America and the UK.

The ability to pitch the same idea in multiple markets also means that you can spread the time and cost of executing the idea in question over more markets, which in turn lets you develop more ideas for the same money and invest more in any given idea.

For most English-language apps/startups with potential international appeal, the UK is likely to become their second largest market after the US.

So if you've gone to the trouble and expense of developing a good marketing idea or story, with potential international appeal, you might as well pitch it in not just the US and Canada but also the UK (and, if possible, Ireland while you're at it).

(And if your budget stretches to pitching stories beyond North America and the British Isles, then Australia should probably be your next market; and if possible, New Zealand while you're at it).

The UK may be what one US politician recently called a "Tier 2" country but when it comes to international media influence it remains very much a Tier 1 country, punching far above its weight.

Just as London is a global financial center, so is it also a global media center – with influence and reach far beyond the UK. A story that originates in the London or UK media will often get picked up not just by the North American media but also travel the world.

UK media like the BBC, *The Guardian*, *The Mail Online* and *The Financial Times* all have sizable audiences and influence in the US and beyond.

Many founders of US startups fail to realize this. Perhaps because Calm's founders were themselves from the UK, though based in San Francisco, they not only realized but acted on it – and reaped the benefits.

Don't forget Canada (as many do)

Canada is a large and affluent market, right next to the US. It has a growing population of over 38 million – similar to California's – and a larger GDP than, for example, Spain.

The Canadian city of Toronto – where I was born – is the third largest by population in (Anglophone) North America, after New York and Los Angeles, and just ahead of Chicago and Houston.

Yet many businesses expanding to the US forget Canada altogether and fail to give the Canadian market a moment's thought. Perhaps due to my Canadian roots, this total neglect of such a prosperous and easily accessible neighboring market always surprises me.

Yes, it's true that Canadians consume a lot of US media but they also consume even more of their own dedicated media.

Unless Canada is your primary market, however, you don't always need to hire a dedicated and specialist Canadian PR. It certainly helps if you can afford to do so but it's not essential.

I normally work with US-based PRs who have existing contacts with the major Canadian media and experience of pitching to them. I also expect them to include pitching to the Canadian media as part of their brief.

If you're doing a poll and asking respondents in both the US and UK, so that you can then pitch it with local interests in both markets, then it may also be worth asking respondents in Canada too – for precisely the same reason.

The "Greater Anglosphere"

The Western Anglosphere these days extends beyond countries where English is the mother tongue.

A global language training company called Education First compiles an English Proficiency Index, ranking countries of non-native English speakers by their levels of English proficiency.

The Netherlands ranks first, while the Scandinavian countries, Germany, Austria and Singapore all make the top 10. If your target customers include Gen Z and Millennials, who are even more likely than their elders in such countries to have fluent English, then there may be a good case for also including all these markets in your definition of the Western Anglosphere.

Even without any marketing in or specifically targeting Germany and/or the Netherlands, these two countries will often appear in the top 10 markets for many English-language apps, while the top dozen or so markets may well also include one or more Scandinavian countries too.

India has a large and fast-growing middle class of proficient English-speakers – which is, indeed, larger than the entire population of many Western countries. Even without giving it any particular marketing attention, India is likely to be among the top 10 markets by traffic of many English-language apps, while South Africa is likely to be in the top 20.

If you can afford to pitch stories in those countries too, they can easily become more valuable markets still.

You can also get US coverage by pitching UK-based media

Something that many don't realize is that, provided you have the right story, you can get plenty of US coverage for a story without ever actually pitching it in the US itself.

Indeed, my experience is that sometimes ideas created and staged in the UK – like the red carpet premiere of *Baa Baa Land* described in the case study below – get more attention in the US and globally than in the UK. (And vice-versa, since I have also executed ideas in the US, which have then, to my surprise at the time, won more attention in the UK.)

This can be because you can instead pitch such stories to US media based in the UK and/or some of the UK media that have sizable US audiences and/or influence, either among Americans in general or perhaps just American media.

Media such as the BBC, *The Guardian, The Daily Mail/Mail Online* and *The Financial Times/ FT.com* all have sizable US audiences.

The likes of *Vogue, Cosmopolitan, Marie Claire* and *Wired* all have editions – both print and online – in both the UK and US, among other markets, and content in/on the UK edition can get picked up by the US edition.

The BBC, in particular, is respected, trusted and widely consumed by Americans. It has a higher "brand trust score," says the latest Reuters Digital Report, than any of the US networks, rolling news channels or national newspapers. It also has the same offline weekly reach as *The Wall Street Journal* and *USA Today* and barely behind *The New York Times*.

It is also disproportionately influential among more educated and liberal Americans, some of whom view it as a sort of antidote to the ever-growing partisanship of much US media, especially some of the rolling news channels.

The result is that if an idea or news story is strong enough and of wide enough interest, you can some-times pitch it just to the media in London and end up having it covered by the US media.

When I worked, for example, with the language company Today Translations in London to place an ad for the world's first emoji translator, the story was first picked up by the BBC World Service and BBC News Online.

Within a few days, however, it had been covered by all the biggest US TV networks, among other major US media – all without us ever pitching it to any US media.

The major US media, of course, also have their own correspondents on the ground in the UK.

So when we staged the world premiere of *Baa Baa Land*, at the Prince Charles cinema in central London, both Reuters and Associated Press, two of the world's three biggest global news agencies, sent London-based TV journalists to cover the event – resulting in huge coverage not just in the US but across the world.

Likewise, when Findmypast, the genealogy website and Think Inc client, released the records of the royal household staff (1526-1924) online, we pitched the story not just to the US media in the US but also to the US media in London.

The news was covered not just by BBC News Online, resulting in considerable US interest, but also by the London staff of Associated Press, the largest American news agency, resulting in even more US coverage.

You can pitch the same story in both the UK and US (and beyond)

You don't have to generate completely separate ideas, stories and content for the US and UK media. Yes, the media in both countries will – other things being equal – tend to prefer stories with some local interest but, if you come up with the right idea or story, it will often work equally well in both countries.

Sometimes you will need to adapt it for each country. So when I conducted a poll for the genealogy website Findmypast, we actually did separate polls, with a separate list of embarrassing place-names in each country. In the event, Toadsuck (Arkansas) topped the US poll, while the Dorset village of Shitterton topped the UK poll – and the media in both countries loved the story.

When we did a poll for Calm to find the most widely held sleep myths in both countries, we asked the same question in both markets but wrote up the results for each one separately.

So we pitched it as a US story, with US data to the US media and a UK story with UK data to the UK media, and, indeed, a French story with French data in France. When it added value, we also highlighted differences between the results in each country.

Other types of stories are of more universal interest and don't need any adaptation. When Think Inc helped the custom fabric website, Spoonflower, celebrate the Queen's 90th birthday by creating a unique tribute of 90 corgi pillows, the story ended up getting more coverage in the US than the UK.

When we made *Baa Baa Land*, and then, as just mentioned, staged its red carpet premiere at a London cinema, both stories, with no need for localization, got at least as much coverage in the US as the UK.

The same was true of two other stories for Calm: when we created *The Lost Grimm Fairytale*, the first bedtime story written by AI, and we turned the EU's new GDPR legislation into a bedtime story, called *Once Upon A GDPR*.

In some cases, such as the ad placed by Think Inc – and mentioned above – for an emoji translator, there's not only no need to *adapt* the idea for US media but you don't even need to pitch it to them, since they will pick it up from UK media and run with it in the US.

It's not just about language

The Western Anglosphere not only shares the same language but also, of course, many of the same morals, anxieties, sensibilities and cultural preoccupations. Or, to put this another way, the cultural divide in the West between the Anglosphere and non-Anglosphere is much clearer than the one between, say, North America and Europe.

James Marriott, a journalist on *The [London] Times* expanded on this theme in a recent column: " ... In a world connected by social media, language not geography is becoming a critical cultural divide. The West, which we are accustomed to thinking of as a monolith, is split between those English-speaking countries that share the internet with America and those that do not."

America's culture wars seem – especially to anyone on Twitter (now X) – almost shared by the rest of Western Anglosphere far more than they do by non-Anglophone Europe.

Many Brits, Canadians and Australians, observed Marriott, now psychologically inhabit an American world and preoccupy themselves with US politics and US Supreme Court decisions.

While American and European cultural concerns seem, observe some commentators, to be diverging, those of the Western Anglosphere are growing ever closer.

CASE STUDY

Our One In-the-Flesh-Stunt: The Red Carpet Premiere of the Dullest Movie Ever Made

"Clad in a sparkling ball gown and tuxedo, the stars of the latest film to premiere in London's Leicester Square walked the red carpet in a rather unusual manner – on four legs."

— Reuters

"Sometimes a thing exists that is so bizarre you just have to shrug and say, 'Sure, why not?'

— IndieWire

When the global buzz generated by the announcement of *Baa Baa Land*, along with the unveiling of its poster and trailer, exceeded even our expectations, we decided to take the risk of coming back three months later for more coverage.

We did so by staging a rare, in-the-flesh stunt – the world premiere of *Baa Baa Land* at the Prince Charles Cinema in the heart of London's West End.

Sheep wearing (comfortably fitting) tuxedos and evening dress walked the red carpet before securing a place in movie immortality by placing their hoof-prints in "cement" [a tray of soft mud] on the world's first "Jollygood Trot of Fame", commemorating such screen legends as "Ram Gosling", "Emmaaa Stone" and "Ewe Grant".

The audience came dressed in pajamas, with dressing gowns/bathrobes and pillows, prepared for a long night.

The cheering crowds of onlookers which jostled for a closer view of the film's stars in the flesh, were, I can reveal here for the first time, largely a rent-a-mob of friends, acquaintances and friends of friends.

A limited number of tickets for the premiere, however, had gone on sale to the public via the Prince Charles Cinema at £7.50 ($10) each.

"We don't expect a big audience," I pronounced to the world's media, in my role as the film's producer. "In fact, we'll be surprised if many turn up at all – and *amazed* if folks stay to the end."

A handful of real customers actually bought tickets for the premiere and unconfirmed reports claim that one or two even stayed until the end.

We staged the premiere on the same day that Calm released the film to a global audience by livestreaming it via its social media channels. For those lacking the time or will to sit through the main, eight-hour feature, we prefaced the main feature with the premiere of a five-minute, condensed version of the full-length film.

It was given to me in my role as the film's producer both to pronounce the event a "shear delight," before adding, "We hope *Baa Baa Land* will be this year's sleeper hit."

This was the only in-person stunt that I have so far staged for Calm.

In an age of shrinking newsrooms, when fewer media have the resources to send journalists to cover stunts in person, you face the growing risk, especially if you're not already a nationally known brand, that few or no media will turn up for such events.

You therefore now generally have to capture the event yourself and share the results with the media and on social.

In this case, however, the risk paid off and the media did turn up and cover it.

The coverage was led by two of the world's three biggest global news agencies – Reuters and AP (Associated Press) – which both sent camera crews.

Reuters also sent a reporter to conduct interviews and then issued no less than three different content packages (two on video and one comprising text and pictures) to its global subscribers and thanked us for "a great story."

The result was another shedload of global buzz and coverage.

RULE TEN: Join the cultural conversation – with reactive, opportunistic, newsjacking ideas

Or, to put this rule another way, you need to join the wider cultural conversation, with ideas that "newsjack" current events and the Zeitgeist itself.

Calm did this brilliantly on at least two occasions, for neither of which can I claim credit.

The first was not strictly a PR idea but a sponsorship deal that involved Calm sponsoring one key element of CNN's 2020 election night coverage of the Trump-Biden contest.

In an impeccably bi-partisan stunt, Calm's logo flashed onto America's screens during CNN's "Key Race Alert" coverage, generating massive buzz – and an impressive spike in downloads – for Calm, while ostensibly also reminding viewers of the need to relax at a moment of peak stress.

Then in the summer of 2021, Calm harnessed both the news and Zeitgeist again, when tennis star Naomi Osaka announced on social media that she would be skipping all news conferences during the French Open to protect her mental health.

When the tournament organizers fined her $15,000 and threatened further sanctions, Osaka asked for her fine to be donated to charity.

Calm promptly stepped in to announce that it would do what the tournament organizers would not and donate $15,000 – equivalent to Osaka's fine – to a French sports charity working to transform the lives and mental health of young people through sport.

It accompanied this donation with a social media campaign declaring that "Mental health is health" – and again won a heap of coverage, buzz and praise for putting its money where its mission was.

"There's a lot of brand love out there for Calm," one senior Calm marketing executive told me recently. "People know and love Calm. We show up in the culture and people like that."

∼

Newsjacking or "reactive PR", is becoming an ever more widely used and important technique.

If you haven't got time to monitor all the news media relevant to your brand, one useful tip for increasing the chances of you noticing news events and stories in time to react to them effectively is to set up RSS feeds for the sort of keywords that will alert you to relevant stories and Google alerts almost as they appear.

Forums like Quora and Reddit are also good places to spot trending niche topics, and when it seems worthwhile, to prepare a suitable reaction or response for pitching to appropriate media.

Reactive PR is hard to do well and easy, in various ways, to get wrong, including by being insensitive, tone-deaf, crass and overly commercial in the sense of trying too hard to plug your brand rather than make a meaningful contribution to the conversation, or just not being quick and/or clever enough.

There is also, as in so many areas, ever more competition to stand out, which, of course, raises the bar for doing it successfully.

But when you do get it right it won't just make you part of the cultural conversation but also help you reach new, different and sometimes much larger audiences than more routine and long-planned ideas.

And the Eleventh Rule?
The biggest limiting
factor is not the subject
or budget but the client

I wasn't sure whether to give this point the status of an eleventh "Golden Rule" but since ten rules seemed a rounder number than 11, plus more like the 10 Commandments, I decided instead to classify it merely as a further observation.

So what almost became Rule 11 states that: the biggest obstacle to winning attention for a brand, in my experience, is not the subject or even the budget but the client – and what they'll let you do.

Or, to put this another way: you're only as good as the ideas that the client will greenlight.

Having some kind of reasonable budget definitely helps but it should be possible, without a huge budget, and if the client will allow you, to win global coverage for a brand making anything from reinforced concrete to aluminum siding.

(And if you happen, in this context, to be your own client, then you need to allow, if not coax yourself, to enlist your more creative and sometimes less serious self and become the kind of client you need.)

One of the best clients that I've ever had was the self-publishing site Lulu, where the COO, to whom I reported, said to me when I started: "You tell me that you're good at this, whereas it's not my area of expertise. I'm therefore going to let you do what is that you do and judge you on the results."

The result was shedloads of coverage and buzz that helped fuel rapid growth and delivered a delighted client.

Some clients, on the other hand, are too stern or serious or too nervous of the frivolous or unorthodox, or simply too cautious to let you do much at all.

One of the worst clients that I've ever had was an ed-tech scaleup, where the exec to whom I reported responded to the ideas that we delivered by forming a sub-committee to evaluate them and posed its members the question: "Can any of you think of any reason for NOT doing any of these ideas?"

There are, of course, always reasons to reject any given idea. The idea without objections does not exist and never will.

The result in this case was that the client did not greenlight *any* of the ideas at all or want any other ideas instead. Everyone's time and money was wasted.

Calm has been a wonderful client to work for, with an openness that many lack towards doing playful and sometimes silly things.

Michael Acton Smith, the co-founder with whom I've worked most closely, has great judgment and instinct for PR and is always fizzing with ideas himself. Both he and Alex Tew have a track record of repeatedly coming up with winning ideas.

It doesn't hurt that Michael is also generous with praise. Indeed, he said to me at one point, "Alex and I think of you as Calm's secret weapon."

This may have been because, with my help, Calm was able to leverage a type of PR, guerrilla marketing and buzz generation that rivals couldn't and didn't.

Then again, it may have just been flattery.

But who was I to argue?

The Buzz Factor: How to Build a Buzzy Brand

How do you become a buzzy, happening, talked-about brand?

The short answer, of course, is that you start by reading this book – which, at this point perhaps you have now largely done.

The longer answer, based on my experience with both Calm and other clients, as well as on observing other brands known for their buzz, is that it has less to do with money than mindset – of both the brand and those who market it.

It is most of all perhaps to do with the right combination of creativity, irreverence, humor, playfulness, fun or silliness, some reasonable tolerance for both risk and failure, and sheer volume of creative output. Enlisting the support of the right celebrities – when possible – doesn't hurt either.

Brands other than Calm that have repeatedly generated more than their share of buzz range from Red
Bull, the energy drink, to Liquid Death, the canned
water startup, and BrewDog, the British craft brewer.

Wrexham AFC, the non-League Welsh football/soccer
club bought by Hollywood stars Ryan Reynolds and Rob
McElhenney, and The Savannah Bananas, the minor
league baseball club in Savannah, Georgia, have both
transformed the fortunes of obscure sports clubs with
the power of buzz.

Money certainly doesn't hurt - Red Bull spends lots -
and nor does having the help of a hot and savvy
Hollywood A-lister like Ryan Reynolds. But the right
sort of guerrilla, light-hearted approach is more readily
available and, in the end counts most of all; and,
anyway, makes whatever budget you do have go
further.

Indeed, the sterner and stuffier that your competitors
behave, the more room that leaves you to stand out by
being playful and irreverent by contrast - and by
consistently doing so, ultimately seeming kind of cool.

Not every idea needs to amuse and/or charm but it
definitely helps if a good proportion are able to do at
least one or the other.

BrewDog has won brand fame with a more punk, abra-
sive and sometimes controversial approach - amid
accusations of a toxic company culture - that may not

have been long on charm but has fitted the brand and delivered loads of buzz.

I tend to think that you can achieve much of the same, however, with a smile on your face and a more amiable vibe.

Indeed, Liquid Death has managed to combine a death metal and neo-punk aura with an environmental message and the impression that it is putting on the whole act with a twinkle in its eye, and in the end, a fairly benign sense of fun.

Some other secrets of becoming a buzzy brand include:

• *Some tolerance for risk*

Not *loads* of risk. And not silly, thoughtless or needless risks but a certain amount of calculated and strategic risk – since, as the novelist Erica Jong once put it, "And the trouble is, if you don't risk anything, you risk even more."

• *Some tolerance for failure*

This means both knowing and accepting in advance that not every idea is going to succeed – and if somehow it does, that probably means that you are not trying anything new or, indeed, taking enough risks.

• *Thinking "media neutral" and "cross-channel"*

If you come up with a good idea, then you should plan to leverage it not just through PR and traditional or "earned media" but also through owned media (your own site, newsletter, podcasts, social channels, etc.) and social media (yours and other people's, including influencers).

Indeed, you should be setting out from the start to generate ideas designed to work across all media and channels.

Traditional media are still powerful and important – and a good piece of media coverage can do wonders for your brand awareness, credibility and growth – but they are also steadily both shrinking in number and in relative, long-term, historical decline compared to the ever-growing reach and influence of both owned and social media.

Some ideas may still work better or only on traditional media and others on social. But the future, as traditional and social media increasingly converge, is "media neutral" and "cross-channel" – and the best, most impactful ideas will work across *all* media.

The one constant – apart from change – is that the brand with the best ideas still wins, while, in the process, still getting the most buzz for its buck.

The idea is still the fuel in the car and the jewel in the crown – and the value and need for creativity is greater than ever.

- *Making your social channels buzzy too*

As well as crafting ideas designed for leveraging across all media channels, it helps if you also create content specifically for social that is lively, fun and amusing in a way that is going to boost engagement, likes, comments and shares.

This is even truer than once, since the fastest-growing social media, like Instagram, and most of all, TikTok, reward entertainment and delight even more than what might now almost be called "legacy" social media, like Facebook and Twitter/X.

On the one hand, this might all sound obvious but on the other hand, it can't be *that* obvious since it's not something that most brands even attempt.

This means that those brands that *do* both attempt and succeed in creating fun and amusing social content, stand to become all the buzzier as a result.

What's the value of being buzzy anyway?

The brand Liquid Death has taken something as commoditized as water and used the power of buzz to build, in a few short years, a business valued – at the time of writing – at $700 million.

Red Bull has gone further and built a $16 billion drinks brand and market leader, without ever making any drinks or owning any manufacturing plants but instead by focusing all its efforts on one thing: generating buzz.

Most people think that Red Bull is a drinks company. It is, in truth, a marketing company and buzz machine – and has become so by setting out from the start to own not factories but eyeballs.

When I worked for Lulu.com, one of the tech giants kept offering to buy it.

The two things that this suitor valued Lulu for, it said, were, second, the community, but, first, the buzz: it just *never* stopped hearing and reading about Lulu.

And the *reason* it valued these things, presumably, is that they were the two things that this would-be buyer couldn't just splash its ample cash on and recreate itself in a matter of weeks.

The buzz for Lulu not only attracted suitors but also helped fuel growth. It became one of the keys to the brand and the business.

Calm also became a buzzy brand in a way that not only helped it stand out from rivals but was also among the things that helped prime its growth, impress investors and boost its valuation.

The value of buzz, what's more, is only likely to grow. In the coming AI revolution, I believe, it will be greater than ever.

We're all struggling to guess the full scale of disruption that ChatGPT, Bard and AI, in general, will bring not just to startups and tech, including many once shiny new "disruptors" themselves, but to brands, businesses and industries of all kinds.

It's probably safe to say, though, that AI will threaten or destroy more brands and businesses than yet realize it, by doing or providing for little or nothing, what they currently charge customers for.

The reason for mentioning this here is that the best defense against this threat for many such brands may well be brand-building and buzz.

"At scale, your company will need some kind of 'moat' to protect it from competitors," wrote Matt Lerner, a startup growth strategist in a recent Linkedin post. "(E.g. valuable patents like Roche, low-cost provider like Walmart, network effects like LinkedIn, or high switching costs like Gmail). Brand can be an incredible moat, but it's expensive and takes years to build."

And the most cost-effective way to build a brand in my opinion is by generating the sort of buzz described in this book.

Is it far-fetched to suggest that building a buzzy, happening, talked-about brand – and the emotional connection with your customers that this brings – might be not just the best but, for many, the only hope for business survival in the great age of AI disruption?

Back to the present, all the brands that I've mentioned here somehow managed to become buzzy, happening and talked-about without the benefit of this book or the 10 Golden Rules of PR and Guerrilla Marketing that it outlines.

Hard to believe, I know, but they did.

You, dear reader, on the other hand, have it easier than any of them. You now have in front of you the rules and manual and key to the buzz factor.

You, in short, have no excuse.

What are you waiting for?

Conclusion

And so, as Porky Pig used to say at the end of the Looney Tune cartoons, that's all folks.

I hope that you've enjoyed reading the story of Calm's journey from nine staff in a one-bed apartment toiling on an app that its founders worried no-one had heard of, to it first becoming Apple's App of the Year and then the first mental health unicorn.

And of how it then became, in what seemed no time all, an app that standups were riffing off to receptive audiences in London comedy clubs and Time magazine was featuring alongside all kinds of household-name brands in its annual list of "100 Most Influential Companies".

I also hope that you've found my "10 Golden Rules of PR and Guerrilla Marketing" not just interesting but

Peter Freedman

useful – and that, if we ever meet, you'll be able to recite them back to me from memory in the correct order.

If not, don't worry, since at the heart of this book are two simple messages:

First, silly PR and marketing are better than serious PR and marketing – and a sense of playfulness and irreverence can take you farther than you might think.

Second, creativity gives you more buzz for your marketing buck.

In an age of information overload and millions of apps and other brands competing in the ever more insanely competitive "attention economy", it's never been tougher to get attention – or more vital.

I wish you good luck in winning your app, startup, scaleup or other brand all the buzz and attention that it needs and deserves.

But then, of course, you no longer need luck, now that you know both my 10 Golden Rules of PR and Guerrilla Marketing and the secrets of becoming a buzzy, happening, talked-about brand.

All you need to do now is *act* on them.

If, however, you're not feeling as lucky or confident as you should be by now, or might just like some help or advice with your efforts, then do get in touch.

I'd be happy to hear from you.

LinkedIn:

https://www.linkedin.com/in/peterfreedman1/

Website:

https://think-inc.co.uk/

Could Your Startup Become Famous? Take This Quick Test to Find Out

Could your app or startup become famous?

My agency, Think Inc, has created a simple way to help you find out.

We've developed a quickfire assessment tool to help you learn if your startup or scaleup is primed and ready to win more than its share of media and social media buzz.

So before reading on, take our simple scorecard, designed to help you answer the question, "Could your startup become famous?"

Take the scorecard at www.think-inc.co.uk/scorecard or scan the QR code below.

It will reveal your app or startup's "Fame Potential Score".

Businesses with "fame potential" are every day landing unpaid media coverage and social media buzz equivalent to millions in free advertising.

The questions are designed to score you in several key areas. Once you answer them, you'll get a customized report and recommendations based on your answers. It will show you where you're already doing well and where you most need to improve.

Take the Think Inc scorecard now and it will tell you straight away both if your brand could become famous – and how to increase your odds of making it so.

• Assessment is 100% free.

• It takes just two to three minutes to complete.

• You will get customized insights instantly

www.think-inc.co.uk/scorecard

SCAN ME

SCAN ME

Acknowledgments

I want to thank all the people who helped me edit, illustrate, design and publish this book and/or who suggested that I write it in the first place.

I owe the greatest thanks to my wife Fiona, for being, among many other admirable things, such an invaluable editor of my writing, including this book, and to my son Ted, both for his many insightful suggestions on the manuscript and all the unpaid and sometimes thankless time that he has put into training me to use fewer ellipses and em-dashes and mentions of the word "meanwhile".

I'm grateful both to Susan MacTavish Best, a long-time friend and former colleague, for first recommending me to Calm and also to Michael Acton Smith and Alex Tew both for hiring me for Calm and then for being such great clients to work for and with. Thanks also in particular to Michael, both for writing the Foreword to this book and for suggesting in the first place that I write the book.

Many thanks to Pete May for helping edit the book and making lots of great suggestions. Having spent many years both editing and enjoying the many articles that he wrote for me in my days as an editor, I knew that he'd be the perfect person with whom to swap roles.

I thank Andrew Priestley for his excellent illustrations after I approached him because I had admired his illustrations for other books. I also thank Valery Gyorgy for her eye-catching cover design and Henry Hyde for his typography and layout of the book's contents.

I thank Niha Imran for helping in multiple ways, including by proofreading and copy-editing the manuscript.

I owe big thanks to my friends Nicholas Schoon, Stephen Fraser and Tricia Beaumont for reading the manuscript and giving loads of excellent feedback and recommendations.

I also want to thank Lucy McCarraher, Joe Gregory and Geraldine Brennan of Rethink Press for much valuable advice and Robin Phillips for his advice on the publishing process.

I also owe great thanks to Todd Brabender for being a vital collaborator on all the work for Calm described in this book and to Christi-an Slomka, Nicholas Head and Enes Alili at Calm for collaborating on many of the ideas described and for each always being a pleasure to work with. I likewise thank Morgan Oliveira for being a great colleague to work alongside.

I thank the multi-talented Garth Thomas, who shot, directed and edited the movie *Baa Baa Land* and Hannah Lifford, who organized and produced its world premiere. Eleanor Kashouris and Anna Kashouris were also each a great help in researching and otherwise helping on multiple projects.

I also want to thank Vinny Pujji, partner at the New York VC firm, Left Lane Capital, whom I have never spoken to or met but whose *Business Breakdown* podcast on *Calm: The Sleeping Giant*, inspired me to write the original long blog post that then became the blueprint for this book.

About the Author

Peter Freedman is the founder of and Director of Thinking at Think Inc, a creative PR, guerrilla and viral marketing agency.

He helps funded startups, scaleups and challenger brands grow faster and win more than their fair share of attention. He helps brands to *keep* winning attention with a production line of new ideas that *keep* delivering fresh buzz, links, traffic, revenue and growth.

He is based in the UK and typically works for clients in both the US and UK at once. He also runs international campaigns across multiple markets.

For the past 18 years, he has worked for startups and scaleups in both the US and UK, typically both at once. He also manages international campaigns across multiple markets.

He has worked for/with everyone from Calm to Craigslist (for 11 years in the US and UK), to Lulu, Badoo, Bloom, Spoonflower, Apple, Disney, Kellogg's, VisitScotland, Marks & Spencer and UNICEF.

He has developed a growing specialty in working for health and mental health brands.

He also helps brands from the UK and Europe expand to the US and vice-versa. He has presented widely to UK businesses on the subject of US expansion and written an eBook called *Heading to America: How to Win Media Attention* – available at www.headingtoamer ica.com/.

His personal goal on any project, however, is to win coverage in the *North Korea Times*, which he has achieved on several occasions.

He also gives webinars, seminars and training on creativity and idea generation.

Before founding Think Inc, Peter was a journalist. He wrote widely for national newspapers and magazines and reported for BBC TV. He has edited both magazines and websites on diverse subjects.

He is also:

- The producer and screenwriter of (as he may have mentioned) *Baa Baa Land*, the "dullest movie ever made."
- The author of the world's first job ad for a specialist "Emoji Translator."
- The commissioning editor of the world's first testicle cookbook – *The Testicle Cookbook: Cooking With Balls* – complete with recipes for

testicle pizza, testicle omelet and bulls' testicles with bechamel sauce.
- The creator of The Blooker Prize, the world's first literary prize for "blooks", or books based on blogs or websites.
- The co-author of the *Socceranto: Birth of A Language* – the invention of a new international language of/for soccer.
- The author of the book, *Heading to America – How to Win Media Coverage*.
- The author of *Glad to be Grey – A Celebration of Dullness*, which *The Guardian* called "brilliant", despite not being invited to the launch party: the first literary launch party held in a coin-op laundromat, when everyone who was no-one was there.

LinkedIn:

https://www.linkedin.com/in/peterfreedman1/

Website:

https://think-inc.co.uk/

Testimonials:

https://www.think-inc.co.uk/praise/

Case studies:

https://www.think-inc.co.uk/work/

Shucks! Some Kind Words About The Author

"He who tooteth not his own horn,

the same shall not be tooted."

Damon Runyon

$$\sim$$

"Peter Freedman is a PR genius and has dreamed up endless stories for Calm."

Michael Acton Smith, co-founder, Calm

"Peter led our 'Silly PR' efforts at Calm and these efforts were a huge part of our success. If you know this space, you know that Peter is a legend."

Anson Whitmer, CEO at Mental, Ex-Head of Data at Calm

"What Think Inc's Peter Freedman does is unique. He is a master at creating online buzz, which spreads globally. He has shown so repeatedly for big brands, like Craigslist and Badoo."

Amit Shafrir, President, Badoo

"I've never met anyone better than Peter Freedman at creating ideas that grab attention and spread virally – often around the world."

Bob Young, CEO, Lulu.com and co-founder, Red Hat

"Many consultants talk about the importance of viral marketing and buzz but Think Inc's Peter Freedman is the only one I've ever met able to deliver on the promise of them."

Stephen Fraser, co-founder, Spoonflower

"Think Inc brought us a scale of attention out of all proportion to cost [...] Peter Freedman is truly a jujitsu master of modern PR."

Gart Davis, co-founder, Spoonflower.com: former President, Lulu

"The Testicle Cookbook has been a huge success: better than we could have imagined... Brilliant!"

Lisa Moore, Marketing Manager, Yudu

"Your work has been fantastic [...] An amazing job."

Leon Mueller, CEO, Bloom

"Thanks for a great job. The US campaign got fantastic pick-up. The place-names story really went viral. Our traffic grew by nearly 600%."

Carolynne Bull-Edwards, Head of PR, Findmypast/Brightsolid

"I never would have believed the amount of coverage you have achieved for us. It has completely knocked me out."

Jurga Zilinskiene, MD, Today Translations

"The job you've done has been fantastic [...] Everything we hoped for."

Caroline Keith, Manager, Consumer Public Relations, Visit Scotland

"Think Inc provides [...] something spookily different – but very deliverable."

Martin Clarkson, Director of Brands, Marks & Spencer

"Think Inc won our launch global coverage by coming up with a great idea that tickled the media and then spread by word of mouth."

Michael Jacobs, CEO, Universal Support

"Think Inc brought us huge global coverage by coming up with quirky ideas and knowing how to execute them [...] The coverage brought us both visitors and high-quality links. It was a uniquely cost-effective form of online marketing."

Richard Stephenson, CEO, Yudu

"Calm grew massively by word-of-mouth and a big part of that was because we knew how to insert ourselves into the cultural conversation.

"It's hard to do this via traditional PR. The better way – especially in the social media age – is by "silly PR".

"Peter led our 'Silly PR' efforts at Calm and these efforts were a huge part of our success."

Anson Whitmer, CEO at Mental, Ex-Head of Data at Calm

"I've worked with many PR folks in my career but Peter Freedman is by far the best and most creative."

Michael Acton Smith, co-founder, Calm

Made in the USA
Las Vegas, NV
22 March 2024

87538118R00111